GRASSINGTON AND WHARFEDALE

A Companion Guide and Souvenir

Illustrated by Neil Wingate   Written by Linden Stafford

First published in 1977
by Linden Stafford and Neil Wingate
Grassington

Printed in Great Britain
by The Craven Herald Ltd
Skipton

ISBN 0 9505497 0 3

Contents

1 INTRODUCTION

Wharfedale, from Bolton Abbey to the source of the Wharfe, is probably the most lovely, unspoilt and varied valley in the whole of England, combining majestic mountains with lush meadows and woodland, harmonious stone-built villages with the freedom of the high moorlands. It has been a source of inspiration to painters and writers, including Turner and Wordsworth. Grassington itself is the ideal centre for the visitor wishing not only to explore the whole area but to absorb the atmosphere of a typical Dales village, while still finding all the necessary amenities for a holiday.

This book is intended both to delight the eye and to be a practical guide for the visitor to Grassington and Wharfedale. Not only will it help to make a holiday here more interesting, but it will also be a permanent reminder of Wharfedale's magnificence. Neil Wingate's illustrations will convey the beauty and character of the scenery and villages of Wharfedale more accurately than can be done in words. The text will attempt to explain why Wharfedale looks as it does today, and what kind of life has been led here from earliest times onwards, as well as pointing out the most worthwhile places to visit and their background. While concentrating on the history, topography and architecture of the area, we shall not neglect Wharfedale's many legends and romances, without which much of the place's character would be lost.

Each chapter will set out in detail a particular excursion from Grassington - a car tour, a short walk or a combination of both. Most of the walks described are on very easy terrain, but the visitor is recommended to obtain an Ordnance Survey map if he wishes to do any serious fell walking. For those who are unable to attempt some of the walks, it should be pointed out that the main places visited on foot can be reached by car too, though clearly to get off the beaten track is always an advantage. Thus we hope to cater for people of all ages, and with all kinds of interests.

BACKGROUND TO WHARFEDALE

To the casual observer, it might seem that Wharfedale has never changed; and it is difficult, too, to imagine a time when livings were not primarily made by pastoral farming, tourism and quarrying. In fact, the landscape exhibits a unique and delightful blend of the natural and the man-made; and throughout the centuries Dalespeople have been involved in a wide variety of activities, from leadmining to textiles, and the lifestyles have been influenced by such forces as the Norman hunting aristocracy and the monastic houses.

Geologically, Wharfedale is dominated by the Great Scar Limestone, with Millstone Grit on the higher fell tops. It is this massive pure limestone that has created the characteristic scenery of the upper dale, where rocky outcrops and scars break through the hill slopes and woodland, and where the beautiful grey stone of the buildings and drystone walls blends into the landscape. Over large areas the surface of the rock has been exposed and then eroded into vast limestone pavements, where a system of deep clefts or joints isolates rectangular blocks or clints like gigantic paving stones. In some places joints have been dissolved into potholes, some of which lead to caves and underground watercourses. It is the Great Scar Limestone that is responsible for such marvellous natural features as Kilnsey Crag, and the Craven Faults in the limestone are demonstrated at Linton Falls near Grassington and lower down at the Strid.

The other major factor in moulding the Wharfedale landscape is the Ice Age, during the latter stages of which the valleys assumed their present steep-sided, flat-bottomed U-shape. Glaciers scoured out the rocks into weird shapes, as at Kilnsey, cut away projecting spurs and stripped rocks bare of soil, carrying the debris down the valley to be deposited as both lateral and terminal moraines. At the end of the Ice Age, terminal moraines that crossed the whole valley acted as dams, impounding lakes which gradually silted up to form rich, flat meadowland. The gravelly moraines were ideal building sites for the first sizeable settlements.

Thus the main formations of Wharfedale were established many thousands of years ago. The development of the vegetation is more complex. By around 5000 BC a great forest, mainly of oak, covered the Dales, the character of which then experienced a series of changes, based on climatic variations. With wetter conditions peat overwhelmed some of the trees on the uplands, and many cliffs remained unforested. Later on prehistoric cultures began the clearance of the virgin forest, and it was not until then that the now common ash woods became plentiful. Thus Wharfedale owes the treelessness of its upland fells both to nature and to settlers.

Little is known about prehistoric man in Wharfedale, though stone circles of the late Stone and Bronze Ages can be seen, and evidence of Bronze and Iron Age settlements

FIELD BARNS NEAR STARBOTTON.

abounds throughout the dale in the form of hut circles and enclosures. Much of the Pennines was the territory of the Brigantes, a hill tribe that attempted to resist the advance of the Romans, who, though victorious, left little trace on the landscape, apart from some remnants of their roads.

It was not until the sixth century that the great settlement of Wharfedale really began, with the coming of the Angles, who spread from the east into the lower parts of the Dales. Soon after, the Danes created other colonies in the same areas, often infilling between existing Anglian settlements. Round about the tenth century the Norsemen invaded from Ireland, settling on the higher fells and further up the valley. The cultures of the Angles and Danes, both arable-farming peoples, gradually merged. By contrast the Norse settlements were scattered, the Norsemen leading semi-nomadic lives passing from one isolated farm to another depending on the season; for theirs was a pastoral economy, based on sheep farming, and having no need of villages. All these invaders eventually settled down peaceably together. However, the different origins of the villages can still clearly be seen: the Anglian villages consist of houses clustered round a central area (now usually the village green) where stock were kept at night, the houses being surrounded by zones first of crofts and enclosures, then of arable fields, then common pastures and finally the moorland 'waste'. Still visible on the ground are Anglian lynchets - terraces cut out to facilitate ploughing with a team of eight oxen on the lower slopes, to augment the arable land on the valley floor. The Norse villages remain as small, isolated hamlets in the remoter uplands.

Wharfedale between the sixth and tenth centuries was thus thickly wooded in the valleys and on the lower slopes - woods that were gradually eroded by the Anglian clearings for settlements and common fields, and by the Norsemen's sheep grazing on the uplands. The endings of the place names reflect the separate ways of life: Anglian *-leah* (now -ley, a clearing) and *-tun* (now -ton, an enclosure and, later, a village); Danish -by and -thorpe (a dependent or outlying farm or hamlet), villages with such endings tending to be situated close to the parent village. The Norse names reflect their economy too: -thwaite (clearing); *-saetr* (now -sett or -side, meaning a shieling); *-skali* (now scale, meaning outlying farm or hut); and topographical features such as fell, beck, gill, mere and moss.

Such were the foundations of most of the villages in Wharfedale, with ways of life that were not on a large scale of production but simply means of survival through some form of self-sufficiency. Such too was the influence on the evolution of the landscape. But with the Norman Conquest a new form of land control was introduced. It was the custom of the Norman aristocracy to reserve large tracts of land for hunting, placing them under special laws which ensured the preservation of game. These vast areas, named Forests - the three examples in Wharfedale being those of Barden, Litton and Langstrothdale Chase - considerably affected the way of life of Dalespeople: within the Forest the number of farms was restricted and sheep grazing was prohibited. The large number of officials required for management, living mainly at the Forest edge, enlarged some villages such as Buckden, whose growth dates entirely from its becoming the headquarters of Langstrothdale Chase. In the upper dale some

Norse sheep farms became Forest lodges, and the Norse settlers were obliged to change their lifestyle from that of shepherds to that of cattle breeders and pig keepers. The removal of land from Forest law was gradual; and with it came the release of land for agriculture and further settlement.

However, from the twelfth century a powerful new influence more or less reversed the effects of the Forest laws. Many monasteries and priories were founded during the twelfth century by the feudal lords, who endowed them with vast tracts of land in the wild uplands of Wharfedale. Being highly skilled in taming the wilderness and in sheep rearing, these monks brought prosperity as well as establishing a new pattern on the land. The economy was managed through granges worked by lay brethren which were either new creations, such as that at Kilnsey, or else, like the Forest lodges, old Norse sheep farms, or even former Forest hamlets. The Cistercian monks of Fountains Abbey owned, among other lands, most of Malham Moor and Littondale, and the Augustinian canons of Bolton Priory were granted numerous estates, particularly in the Barden area. Apart from their skill in the sheep-rearing and wool trade, they ran farms, corn mills and even lead mines. The monks removed many acres of woodland, and the open fells of today are probably largely due to the clearances of monastic days.

The system of green roads in Wharfedale owes much to the granting of markets to feudal lords. Such market towns quickly became prosperous, and were soon linked with other towns and villages by a vast network of packhorse trails, many of which survive today as green roads, most being of a very early date indeed. The development of the market roads also led to the rebuilding in stone of the Wharfedale bridges, most dating from the seventeenth century and originally packhorse bridges, subsequently widened. Other green roads and bridleways were monastic roads, such as Mastiles Lane (see p. 33). In the seventeenth and eighteenth centuries developed the green drove roads used to move cattle from Scotland for fattening in northern England on their way to the southern fairs. The droving traded ended - as did the use of the market roads - in the nineteenth century when the railways and the turnpike roads had created new markets that could more easily be reached.

Perhaps one of the features of the Dales that distinguishes them most from other areas is the presence of drystone walls, patterning the lower slopes and snaking high up the fellsides and over the moorland. Up to the eighteenth century agriculture was based on strip arable farming and on grazing on the common pastures. Where the common pasture was poor, it might be enclosed so that improvements could be made and grazing regulated (such as the sixteenth-century 'New Close' at Conistone). Some other early small walled enclosures were built prior to the eighteenth century, mainly to mark property boundaries or to keep in the livestock. Intakes made around farms by individuals can easily be recognised as irregular enclosures with crooked walls. However, the majority of the walls belong to the period between 1780 and 1820 when the Enclosure Acts caused the break-up of the old system of common fields and the redistribution of the land. On the valley bottoms and lower slopes are rectangular enclosures, and the nineteenth-century walls, planned on paper, run in straight lines for miles across the uplands.

Now the pattern of farming has totally changed. Arable farming - essential in the past for self-sufficiency - has given way to the more economically viable pastoral farming, mainly sheep (shaggy moorland breeds such as Swaledales and Dalesbreds), with a few cattle. The farm buildings have become more centralized with the advent of the tractor, and the field barns scattered across the fellsides are now largely redundant (see p. 63).

Of Wharfedale's industrial past, a few relics remain. Water-powered manorial corn mills were converted for textiles, which prospered until steam power in the West Riding and East Lancashire made them obsolete. The decline of the local textile industry coincided in many places with the decline in leadmining - an industry that had begun in pre-Roman times, flourishing throughout the eighteenth and nineteenth centuries until it ceased to be practical or profitable. The industrial archaeology and its background are described in detail in many of the chapters that follow.

As for the vernacular architecture of Wharfedale, the 'typical Dales house' is the long house - built on a long rectangular plan, with a low-pitched, stone-slate roof, mullioned windows and carved and dated door lintels. Most of the existing buildings belong to the seventeenth or eighteenth century. The mullioned windows were a Tudor fashion adopted rather late by local masons; but the long-house plan is based on the cruck structure introduced by the Anglo-Danish settlers where the bay formed by a pair of crucks became the basic building unit, to be multiplied side by side wherever extra accommodation or space for livestock was required. This long-house style persisted even when houses began to be built in stone, the plentiful supply of which ensured its wholesale use for walls and roofing. Many yeoman farmers embellished the seventeenth-century plan, rebuilding the façade and adding a central doorway, sometimes with a classical pediment, and replacing the mullions with Georgian sash windows at the front of the house.

Such, then, has been the evolution of Wharfedale: a basic limestone formation modified by a variety of factors. Lifestyles have been changed from early self-sufficiency by a series of different administrations, the land finally passing into the hands of the great landowners such as the Dukes of Devonshire and being governed by a number of statutory bodies such as central and local government, and the Yorkshire Dales National Park. Future development is now in the hands of our present-day organizations, and Wharfedale will doubtless continue to evolve in some way, as it has done throughout the centuries.

BACKGROUND TO GRASSINGTON

'Standing healthily high on a gently sloping limestone terrace or shelf, Grassington's position full in the sun on the southern slope of the dale is, for Craven-land, unique. The sun's rays light up early and till late gladden the hearts and quicken to fuller life the bodies of its people, natives and visitors alike. There is medically now that it has a good water supply and electric light! much to be said of a residence here, as already many town-dwellers have proved.' Thus Edmund Bogg, writing in the early 1900s. And despite the quaint hyperbole, this statement still basically holds true.

Grassington's history begins in prehistoric times: evidence

HELMS
GRASSINGTON SQUARE
NEIL WINGATE

of Bronze and Iron Age settlement exists on Lea Green above the present-day village (see p. 40), where the Brigantian rebels retreated from the Romans, who themselves did not make a camp here, though a Roman road from Bainbridge to Ilkley once crossed the higher part of the village. The modern Grassington, however, dates from the sixth century AD when the Anglian invaders settled below the ancient site, building their primitive dwellings on the morainic shelf above the Wharfe, on either side of a beck which used to flow through the centre of the square. It is believed that the position of the original village corresponded to the present Main Street and Garrs Lane. The village's name might be derived from *garrs-tun* (*garrs* meaning enclosures) or or from *gaers-tun* (a grass enclosure); other authorities maintain that Grassington meant 'grazing land', or that Garrs was a proper name. The local pronunciation, 'Girston', suggests at least that 'Garrston' was its name at one time.

Little is known of Grassington before the Norman Conquest, apart from an entry in the Domesday Book of 1086 when the number of families living here was estimated at twelve. The manor, after passing through the hands of the Percys, the Plumptons, the Earls of Cumberland and the Cliffords of Skipton, finally descended to the Dukes of Devonshire. Grassington's importance would have been greatly increased by the granting in 1282 of a charter for a weekly market and an annual fair of three days. The fair still survives as Grassington Feast, held in October, though not on its former lavish scale.

The great rise in Grassington's population coincided with the growth of the leadmining industry on Grassington Moor in the eighteenth and nineteenth centuries (see Chapter 3). A large number of families emigrated to Grassington from as far away as Derbyshire and Cornwall, and many new houses were built and larger houses converted to accommodate this increase. The mining population included blacksmiths, carriers, carpenters, cloggers and cordwainers. From about 1790 there was also an expansion in the textile industry, which had taken over many old water-powered corn mills (see p. 22). But, with the advent of steam power, local mills became redundant, textile-working families moved away, and by the end of the nineteenth century the mills had closed. At about the same time further leadmining was proving uneconomical, the mines were closed, and more families left the area. By the beginning of the twentieth century the population had slumped to 494, whereupon a steady increase began again on account of the opening of the Yorkshire Dales Railway to Threshfield in 1901. Visitors started to arrive and some eventually settled, finding work in the nearby towns or in the rapidly developing limestone quarries. Many of the empty miners' cottages were bought and restored, and the population has now regained its mid-nineteenth-century peak level of around 1100.

Grassington has always been the largest village in Upper Wharfedale. Two very old roads met here - the monastic road from Fountains Abbey to the Lake District (see p. 72) and the road from Skipton to Wensleydale. Today Grassington is easily accessible and, both for its superb situation in the heart of the spectacular scenery of Wharfedale, and for the amenities it has to offer, is unrivalled among Dales villages.

2 A WALK ROUND GRASSINGTON

Walk: allow $1\frac{1}{2}$ hours

Standing in the **square**, one is at the very heart of the ancient Anglian colony first built in the sixth century as a cluster of primitive dwellings surrounding this central space, through which flowed a small beck. Although the stream has now been covered over and the space is no longer a green, this is still the hub of twentieth-century Grassington, as it has been throughout the centuries. There are no longer the weekly markets that began in the thirteenth century; yet the annual fairs are still commemorated in the small fair still held here every October, as part of the traditional Grassington Feast.

This is not the only reason why the square is the best place to begin a town walk. From here one has a splendid view of the Main Street stretching steeply up the hill - described by Pevsner as an 'exceptionally attractive village street' - and here one also gains a general impression of the distinctive character of Grassington. Built mainly in local stone, the centre of the village has a harmonious appearance - each of the buildings and small side streets, despite their variety, blending in with one another. Although many houses have datestones above the doors bearing seventeenth-century dates, most have been altered and extended at a later date, and the central buildings belong in the main to the eighteenth century, the period when the expansion of the village began through the rise of the leadmining industry. A particular feature of Grassington is its many 'folds'. These were originally small crofts running back from the main street, and attached to individual houses; they were gradually filled in with newer cottages as the village expanded in the eighteenth and nineteenth centuries.

The square itself was recobbled in 1973 and contains an old pump. Facing down the Main Street is a fine Georgian-fronted building, formerly the Cafe Royal and, earlier, the Liverpool Warehouse. On the right, at the lower end of the square, is the typically Georgian building of **Grassington House**, built in 1760 by a Mr Brown, one of the promoters of the Grassington to Pateley Bridge turnpike. The characteristic eighteenth-century features are the high sash windows, the central doorway and the symmetrical arrangement of the windows.

Taking the right-hand fork up from the square, Garrs Lane, we pass the Black Horse Inn (a former coaching inn) on the right, at the end of which are the premises of the local **folk museum** – well worth a visit for its accumulation of fascinating local antiquities which relate Grassington and Wharfedale's recent past in visual form. Near the top of Garrs Lane on the right is the **Congregational Church** which, built in 1812, was the earliest Nonconformist church in Grassington. On the left at the top is 'Theatre Cottage', converted from a barn which was used in the nineteenth century as a **theatre**. This was managed by Tom Airey (1771–1842), the local postmaster and carrier between Grassington and Skipton, who, after a brief acting career in Skipton, formed a theatre company in Grassington which eventually established itself in this barn. Edmund Kean and Harriet Mellon are reputed to have acted there in 1807. The theatre was disbanded around the mid-1830s, whereupon Tom Airey took up the mail-coach business, afterwards continued by his family into the late nineteenth century as a daily horse-bus service between Grassington and Skipton.

A cobbled lane leads off left before Garrs Lane meets Scar Street. Here, on the left-hand side, is a remarkable seventeenth-century barn called **Pletts Barn** - known locally as Wesley's Barn owing to the fact that Wesley is said to have preached here on his first visit to Grassington. In the wall to the left of the entry porch are arched ventilation slits, which, together with the pigeon cotes on the right end of the porch, form an attractive pattern on the front of this barn. Nesting boxes were built into the wall (still used by pigeons today!) and there are still the remains of an old pegged oak door.

Continuing along this lane, we soon arrive at the small car park opposite the **Town Hall**, built in 1885 as the Mechanics' Institute and later taken over by the Devonshire Institute. It is now used for various recreational activities as well as parish council meetings, lectures, and so forth. The site on which it stands was once the pinfold where straying cattle were impounded by the village 'pinder'. At the top of the Main Street on the left is the **Dales Centre**, where excursions and lectures on the area are organized. A detour to the right of the Town Hall along Low Lane is well worthwhile; for in a short distance a striking prospect of Grassington's varied roofscape opens out below the lane.

After returning to the Town Hall, we now cross over Moor Lane (leading to Grassington Moor and its lead mines) and continue straight ahead into Chapel Street, comprising

PLETTS BARN.

NEIL WINGATE.

houses mainly of the nineteenth century when the lead-mining industry was at its peak. Passing Intake Lane, Hill Top Fold and the Methodists' Chapel on the right, we reach a group of earlier buildings, among which The Nook and Inglenook are dated 1628 and, though incorporating many later alterations, still retain some seventeenth-century features. The most imposing building at the end of Chapel Street is **Town Head Farm**, a handsome seventeenth-century building now belonging to the Trustees of Fountaine Hospital in Linton, which, with its extensive farming lands between Grassington and Conistone, provides income for the Linton almshouses (see p. 24). It has a two-storeyed porch, and the main part of the house has mullioned windows of three and four lights. On the outer walls, below the roof, some original plaster and stucco decoration can be seen, and the old barn adjacent to the farmhouse has pigeon cotes beneath the eaves.

At Town Head we turn left and left again along Garrs End Lane, which provides an excellent vantage point for a magnificent view up the dale, with the dark green of Grass Wood stretching down to the Wharfe. Opposite the end of Moody Sty Lane are two folds, and we now take the first one, **Chapel Fold**, leading past the former Primitive Methodists' Chapel of 1837, now used as a dwelling and cabinet maker's workshop. This lane was formerly known as Ranters' Fold, after the nickname given to the early Primitive Methodists.

This brings us into Chapel Street, where we bear right just before the Top Shop into the attractive cobbled lane, **Chamber End Fold**. The top house, which dates from the seventeenth century, with eighteenth- and nineteenth-century alterations (such as its Georgian sash windows), has in the top storey a stepped three-light window, and is believed by some to have been the former court 'chamber', thus giving its name to the fold. The cottages lower down were built during the late seventeenth and early eighteenth centuries, probably converted into smaller miners' cottages during the nineteenth-century expansion.

At the bottom of Chamber End Fold we bear left into another old street called Leylands, and from the right-hand side of this follow an ancient and intriguing right-of-way (older than the surrounding buildings) called **The Woggins**. We emerge through an archway under the old pharmacy into the Main Street, at a point known as Neddy Hill.

Further down the Main Street on the right is the site of **Tom Lee's Smiddy**. Tom Lee is Grassington's notorious murderer, about whom many romanticized anecdotes have been written. He was a local blacksmith who in 1766 killed a certain apothecary Dr Richard Petty, after a quarrel in the Anglers Arms at Kilnsey. According to the innumerable versions of the story, Tom Lee waylaid Dr Petty in Grass Wood on his way back from Kilnsey, murdered him and eventually threw the body into the Wharfe at Loup Scar near Burnsall; two years later his assistant (who had been sworn to secrecy) confessed, and Lee was arrested, hanged at York and his body gibbeted at a point near Grass Wood where the murder had taken place.

Lower down still on the left, an old right-of-way called Lucy leads by the Foresters Arms to Garrs Lane, and on the right another fold, Ashfield, leads to **Ashfield House**

CHAMBER END FOLD.

NEIL WINGATE

GRASSINGTON MAIN STREET.

(tucked away right at the end), a pleasing late seventeenth- or early eighteenth-century building with mullioned windows.

Continuing down the hill, past the Devonshire Hotel, an old coaching inn, we reach Jacob's Fold (opposite the pump), leading to yet another ancient right-of-way called Jakey, which passes the **Old Hall** and its grounds. Unfortunately, no extensive view of the hall can be obtained by the visitor, though it is, in Pevsner's terms, 'a remarkable survival', being reputedly the oldest inhabited house in Wharfedale. The building, though much modified in the sixteenth and seventeenth centuries, was founded on a thirteenth-century hall built by Robert de Plumpton as a hunting lodge. The oldest part is the central portion, locally believed to have been a chapel, which is entered from the south by a small pointed doorway. The lower storey has a Tudor mullioned window of five lights, above which are two transomed windows, each of two lights joined together by quatrefoil tracery work. The two later wings built on to each side, with both mullioned and lancet windows, contain much nineteenth-century work. It is possible that the existing hall occupies the site of an even earlier hall, of Norman origins, which would have been demolished when the lodge was built in the thirteenth century.

Jakey brings us out at the Lodge guest house on Wood Lane, where we turn left and left again back into the Main Street, catching a glimpse to the left on the corner of a fine Venetian window at the back of the baker's shop. On the way back to the square, on the right-hand side, is the old **Smithy,** used as such well into this century.

The very attractive building on the left just before the square is known as **Church House**, at one time Chapman's Temperance Hotel, and originally a farmhouse built at the end of the seventeenth century as evidenced by the datestone above the door which bears an unusually carved inscription SAP 1694. Although a Georgian sash window has been inserted on the first floor, Church House still displays many seventeenth-century features, such as the mullioned windows on the ground floor and the continuous drip moulding above them. It is a remarkably fine example of a yeoman's house of the seventeenth to eighteenth century.

The route leads us in a few yards back into the square. However, if the visitor has time for a longer walk, a detour can be made down to **Grassington Bridge**, which is reached by turning right out of Wood Lane and continuing down the hill. Otherwise, the bridge is included in the walk described in Chapter 4. Grassington Bridge (properly called Linton Bridge) replaced in 1603 a derelict wooden structure and is the oldest existing bridge over the Upper Wharfe. However, the original stone bridge was humpbacked, designed for packhorses, so, having already been repaired in 1661, it was widened in 1783 and eventually raised to its present level in 1824. Underneath the bridge two stages of building can be seen: the curvature of the old part downstream is not identical to that of the new, upstream part. On the face of the bridge, on the downstream side, the old line of the humpback is visible, with long, flat triangles of later masonry filling up the dip at each end. The older, downstream part also bears mason marks, identifying the work of different masons.

3 LEADMINING

The vanished leadmining industry is perhaps the most important event in Grassington's history, providing, as it did, much work for local people throughout the eighteenth and nineteenth centuries, and causing whole families to migrate to the Grassington area in search of employment. During this time the Grassington population swelled to a previously unknown peak, and new houses were built and old houses converted to provide extra accommodation.

For those who have an interest in industrial archaeology, the best way of seeing and learning about the background of the existing remains is to take part in one of the interpretative excursions organized by the Dales Centre in Grassington: parties of visitors are taken on to Grassington Moor and guided round the extensive site. Otherwise, a brief trip to Yarnbury or even to Hebden Gill too (see Chapter 6) can give a good general impression.

In the Wharfedale Great Scar Limestone lead ores occur in fissures in rocks mainly as ribbon deposits such as the Grassington–Greenhow Bycliffe vein of nine miles' length. Apart from these extensive mining fields, fringe deposits exist throughout the dale. Both levels and shafts have been used to reach the lead ore, and a series of smelting methods have been employed over the centuries to separate the concentrated lead from the deposit in which it is found.

Its history in the Grassington area dates back to before the Roman occupation; there was some leadmining possibly as early as the Bronze Age, though no such evidence exists in Yorkshire. The earliest reference is to the fact that, after the Roman defeat of the Brigantes in AD 74, some Brigantian prisoners were sent to work in the lead mines on Greenhow Hill (see p. 79), pointing to an existence of lead-mining in pre-Roman times. The early mine workings were rough and unplanned, yielding little lead ore. From the Elizabethan period on, mining began on a larger scale: the Earls of Cumberland in Wharfedale employed agents with special knowledge of mining to make improvements; in the Grassington field, around 1603, miners were brought in from Derbyshire to open and extend the mines at Yarnbury and on Grassington Moor, and a smelt mill was built on the riverside near Low Mill (see p. 22). The earliest primitive shafts can now be seen in the form of bell pits - hollows spreading chain-like along the line of a vein. These mostly belong to the seventeenth and eighteenth centuries, though some may be even earlier. Eventually the shafts became larger and more widely spaced along the vein.

It was not until the 1730s that the real period of expansion began for deeper mining and better drainage on Grassington Moor. During the last quarter of the eighteenth century new methods and mechanization were tried out. Large companies were formed which could afford to spend capital on development and prospecting: long levels were driven in the hopes of discovering veins not visible on the surface and specialist mining engineers worked as agents and managers. In 1779 Cornelius Flint of Derbyshire was sent to Grassington as agent for all the Duke of Devonshire's Yorkshire mines. At a time when drainage of the deeper mines was becoming a problem, Flint began the Duke's Level in 1792 which, when completed some thirty years later, made an increased depth of ground available to be worked. In 1792 Flint also began to replace the primitive ore hearths with reverbatory furnaces (cupola smelting). Again a water problem developed. Water was needed to drive the large wheels for winding shafts, and also for the ore-dressing floors. Thus a system called the Duke's Watercourse was created - a canal of over six miles in length connecting the newly constructed Blea Beck Dams with the whole mining field.

The Duke of Devonshire's mines survived all the major depressions to enter a boom period in the 1840s and 1850s. By the 1850s an extended flue system with condensers had been built to disperse the poisonous fumes and to create a draught for the reverbatory furnace; this rose 150 feet up the slope of the moor to the foot of a 60-foot-high chimney. The Duke's New Road was built across Hebden Gill to link Yarnbury more directly with the Cupola chimney.

At this time production was near its highest ever, but by 1857 the decline had begun; by 1883 all the work both underground and on the surface had been completed. Most of the larger veins had become almost exhausted, and more costly work was required. Also, abundant lead supplies from abroad kept the price too low for the English mines to be able to compete successfully. After the closure of the underground workings nothing more was done apart from the reworking of some of the spoil heaps for valuable minerals found in association with the lead ore: in the 1960s the Dales Chemical Company reworked the mine tips by flotation treatment of the debris.

The life of the miners was a hard and hazardous one, depending through most of the nineteenth century on a system of bargaining. Though miners from Derbyshire and Cornwall flocked to the area, wages were low and erratic and the work unhealthy. Many miners sought to obtain a small croft or 'intake' which they might eventually be able to develop into a smallholding: this not only helped to raise their standard of living but also provided some healthy outdoor exercise. The word 'intake' survives in many street or house names, and evidence of these crofts can be seen all over the moors. The miners were governed by 'laws and customs' first introduced by the Derbyshire miners and drawn up by a 'Barmoot Court' in 1642. The barmaster measured the ground discovered by each miner and two 'meers' were granted to each one. In 1737 a Great Barmoot Court revised the 'laws and customs', and the length of the meer was increased from 21 to 30 yards. In 1764 there was a further review of the laws, and after this stones instead of stakes were used to mark the miners' meers; these meer-stones can still be seen, varying between those with only initials and those with a full name on them - from roughly cut to well-lettered and well-shaped stones - to a few which bear only a number.

The main relics to be seen are the attractive group of administrative buildings at Yarnbury (see p. 38), the Cupola smelt mill chimney (a prominent landmark), the deep air shaft to the Duke's Level in the quarry behind the Cupola chimney, the Duke's Watercourse (mainly overgrown), and something of the system of flues which can still be seen, caved in or partly buried in the ground.

4 ROUND LINTON

Walk: allow 2 hours
Although Grassington owed its population growth to lead-mining, there was yet another industry that provided local people with work and attracted families from outside the area: textiles. This walk is one of the richest in historical interest in the Grassington area, since not only does it take us through the great textile centre of Upper Wharfedale but also includes a parish church that served four villages and the delightful village of Linton itself. Embracing parts of Grassington, Linton and Threshfield, this walk thus offers a view of a central and vital part of the parish of Linton.

The walk begins at the Hebden road where, just past the car park, Sedber Lane leads off to the right. The right-hand pavement takes us into the **Snake Walk** (or Flags), which was part of the old church path from Grassington to Linton Church, descending steeply between two walls down to Linton Falls, the Tin Bridge and Linton Mill.

Linton Falls are caused by the North Craven Fault, which, having passed through Malham Cove and Gordale Scar, crosses the Wharfe at this point, creating a steep drop in the river bed. Underneath the bridge the exposed limestone rocks are horizontal, but a little way downstream the river bed is tilted. Below this the bank is made up of grey shale, more recent in age than the limestone. The Falls are a tremendous sight, particularly when the river is in spate, when the Wharfe thunders over the rocks beneath and beyond the bridge. The **Tin Bridge** itself replaced an earlier structure that had been washed away at the turn of the century during one of the many floods.

Across the bridge, the present **Linton Mill** was built in 1901–2 on the site of earlier buildings. Originally Linton's manorial corn mill using water from Captain Beck (the confluence of Linton and Threshfield Becks), when corn ceased to be ground here in the eighteenth century (on account of the availability of flour from Skipton), Linton Mill was rebuilt for spinning worsteds and, after 1840, cotton, and by the mid-nineteenth century housed a cotton-weaving industry. To serve this larger mill two dams were built across the Wharfe to increase the storage. With the decline in local textiles - due to the growth of steam-powered mills in the West Riding and East Lancashire - the mill became the Linton Falls Creamery, was burnt down, rebuilt and finally used as a cotton-and-rayon-weaving shed until its closure in 1959.

Bearing round Linton Mill, we turn left at the road to Linton Church, which passes two rows of cottages known as **Botany**, a hamlet built around 1850 to house the mill workers. The front row was rebuilt some years ago and the back row has been modernized. Botany is an old West Riding name for houses round a textile mill, possibly derived from Botany wool. The original water supply for these cottages is the strong spring seen in the car park opposite.

The house at the church gate, Kirk Yett, was formerly an inn, though since rebuilt. **Linton Church** is dedicated to St Michael and All Angels and serves the four villages of Grassington, Linton, Hebden and Threshfield. Four 'church paths' led from each village to this central point and still partly survive in the form of footpaths, bridleways, stepping stones, bridges and modern motor roads. The site dates back at least to Danish times: the dedication was frequently given in the seventh century to pagan sites; and its isolated position in the bend of the river tends to support this hypothesis. However, the earliest part of the existing building is Norman - the two eastermost bays of the north aisle of the nave, with their rounded arches. During the fourteenth century the original Norman church was extended east and west, and the exterior walls are of the fifteenth century. There was further enlargement in the sixteenth century, and much restoration in 1861, when a pre-Reformation stone altar was discovered which has since been put into use, and when the clerestory and porch were added and the short, square, thirteenth-century bell-turret was moved (for the third time). Near the south door is a Norman 'tub' font, and on one of the pillars in the south arcade is a small brass crucifix, dating back to the ninth or tenth century; this was found in Linton Beck in 1835, and is probably not English. Up to 1866 Linton Church had two rectors, each with a parsonage in Linton.

At the far corner of the churchyard is a gate, from which a footpath leads to stepping stones across the Wharfe, believed to be part of the church path from Hebden. **Grassington Low Mill**, across the river, again was built on the site of a water-powered corn mill, where a dam was built between a spring, Brow Well, and the river. Here too, textiles took over - worsted, cotton, silk and flax spinning - and, after being used for soap making and furniture, it was finally converted to residential use. During the seventeenth century a smelt

LINTON FALLS

mill was built nearby on the river bank and until 1790 used water from Brow Well; fragments of wall and traces of the wheelpit still exist to the left of Low Mill as viewed from here.

We now return back down the church road as far as a house on the left, where a narrow walled and fenced footpath climbs up to the Burnsall–Threshfield road; here we turn right and then take the left fork into Linton village.

LINTON. The name Linton probably means 'flax enclosure' from Anglo-Saxon *lin* (flax) and Anglian *-tun* (enclosure); or else 'enclosure by the lake', from Old English *hlynn*, meaning pool or torrent. The village was built on a firm glacial moraine, debris left across and along the sides of the valley at the end of the Ice Age, which dammed Linton Beck, causing a shallow lake to spread out towards Cracoe. This glacial lake persisted as marshland, ideal for flax growing, until it was drained around 1850. As late as 1812 flax was still being grown here, thus adding a further dimension to the local textile trade. Linton's formation is typically Anglian - a central green around which most of the houses are clustered. In 1949 it was chosen in a competition as the 'prettiest village in the North'. Not surprisingly - for Linton is unique in that its beck bisects the green and is crossed by fords, stepping stones and three bridges; and although the buildings date from the seventeenth century to the present and display a variety of architectural features, all are stone-built, creating a general impression of harmony.

The **packhorse bridge** dates from the fourteenth century, with parapets that were probably added in the seventeenth century. Adjacent to one of the fords at the far end of the village is the **clapper bridge**, the simplest and probably the oldest bridge here. It formerly stood at the opposite end of the village, beyond the road bridge where there are now stepping stones. When the main road bridge was built in 1892 to replace two fords by which the old road crossed Linton Beck, the clapper bridge was moved to its present site, and, more recently, railings were added and the old flags covered over with tarmac.

The most notable buildings can be seen along the route we now take through Linton, and it is also well worth looking out for attractively carved datestones along the way. On entering the village, we pass the post office on the right which, despite eighteenth-century alterations, still retains its early seventeenth-century plan. Opposite is the old **Manor House**, now two cottages. We now take the road parallel to the beck on the left-hand side. Set back from the road is the **old rectory** (now a youth hostel), which was the rectory for Linton parish until 1930. Its seventeenth-century origins are mainly obscured by eighteenth- and nineteenth-century extensions and alterations. In the right-hand corner of the garden was the second rectory. On the corner of the lane just beyond the youth hostel is the old post office which has a beautiful 1679 datestone over the side door.

Crossing the clapper bridge, we reach the most prominent building in Linton, **Fountaine Hospital** - quite unlike any other building in Wharfedale. Founded and endowed in 1721 by the will of Richard Fountaine for 'six poor men or women', it is reputed to have been designed by Sir John Vanbrugh. The central block comprises a chapel and an elaborate entry surmounted by a square tower and cupola;

LINTON CHURCH AND LOW MILL.

LINTON VILLAGE.

projecting and cross wings contain the almshouses themselves. The east window of the chapel is Venetian, as is the window above the doorway leading to the chapel. With 'a general sense of grandeur' (Pevsner) and its unusual classical design, Fountaine Hospital dominates the village, yet with its Georgian features blends in with the other buildings. Between the Hospital and the beck was the pinfold for straying animals. The income for the almshouses is derived, through the Fountaine Trust, from about 400 acres of land in Grassington.

Keeping the green on our right, we continue past the inn, named after Richard Fountaine, until we reach the main road where, opposite and slightly to the left, stands the **Old Hall**. Its oldest part - the left-hand (western) end with its mullioned windows - was built in the late seventeenth century, two storeys high; some of the mullions were removed to enlarge the windows. Part of the older building was replaced by a three-storey Georgian extension and a handsome eighteenth-century porch with a gable and a pedimented doorway.

To the right, just before the road bridge, a lane leads off to the left along the beckside, from which two buildings of note are visible. On the left, set back among the trees, is **Linton House**, a fine Georgian-fronted seventeenth-century house. Opposite, across the beck, is **White Abbey** (formerly Troutbeck), once the home of the author Halliwell Sutcliffe. Though first built as a typical seventeenth-century yeoman's house, with mullioned windows, considerable nineteenth-century extensions have changed its character at the back.

We should now return to the road bridge, cross it and, passing the post office, take the left fork out of the village. After crossing the Burnsall road to take the road back down to Linton Falls, avoiding the turn-off to the left, we continue on down across the Linton Church road towards the Falls. Instead of turning right, we bear left over **Lile Emily's Bridge**, a quaint little humpbacked footbridge dating possibly from the fourteenth century. It spans Captain Beck (the boundary between Linton and Threshfield) and is probably part of the old church path from Threshfield.

Our footpath follows the river, passing, on the left, the three houses converted from **Threshfield Mill**. This other former manorial corn mill continued the longest of the three to grind corn - right up to the nineteenth century - although it was rebuilt in the seventeenth century. But by the opening of the twentieth century it was a creamery and was eventually altered into the present dwellings. However, the rock-cut goit from Captain Beck can still be traced, and the dam, long since drained, survives as a sunken garden. We now pass the old electricity **power house** on the right, operated from the early twentieth century by water wheel and turbine from the dams that served Linton Mill, until the Electricity Board took over the supply.

Where the riverside footpath joins the main road, we walk left for about 100 yards along the road. This detour is well worthwhile, for on the right-hand side is a superb seventeenth-century school - **Threshfield Free Grammar School** - founded and endowed in 1674 by the will of the Rev. Matthew Hewitt, one of the two rectors of Linton. With its mullioned windows and its two-storeyed gabled porch at the left end containing, in the upper floor, a stepped three-light window, Threshfield School demonstrates Dales architecture at its best. In 1876 it ceased to be a grammar school and is now a primary school. Apart from having architectural merit, the school has a ghost, Old Pam the Fiddler, with whom many legends are associated. In some accounts, he is said to be the ghost of a former fiddler-schoolmaster, murdered by a rector of Linton! According to one tale, Old Pam was often seen in the upper room of the porch fiddling to the schoolchildren, and one night a man who was watching this scene sneezed, was overheard and then pursued down the road by Old Pam and his followers. He escaped by jumping into the Lady Well, where they dared not touch him.

Leaving Threshfield School and its ghost behind us, we retrace our steps and continue to the end of the road as far as **Lady Well Cottage**, built, like Grassington Bridge, in 1603. This house has the characteristic seventeenth-century windows but the pitch of the roof is steeper than is usual in Dales cottages, suggesting that at one time it might have been thatched, and the slates are Welsh rather than of Yorkshire stone. Between this and the neighbouring cottage is a narrow lane leading to **Lady Well**, a spring which runs powerfully even when the river is low, and which was formerly the water supply for all the cottages on this road.

We now cross Grassington Bridge, described on p. 17. Across the bridge, near the footpath up the fields on the left, are good examples of lynchets (medieval ploughing terraces). If we continue up the hill, we re-enter Grassington.

5 THRESHFIELD AND MASTILES LANE

Car tour plus walks: allow 3½ *hours*
This excursion takes in Grassington's neighbour in Linton parish, Threshfield, together with its outlying hamlet, Skyrethorns; and it also includes a Bronze Age stone circle and a short walk on an ancient monastic route.

The visitor should drive to Threshfield and park the car before taking a brief stroll round what remains of old Threshfield.

THRESHFIELD. Like Grassington and Linton, Threshfield too is an Anglian settlement built on a glacial moraine on the side of the valley. Despite recent developments, the heart of old Threshfield still remains. It was never, like Grassington and Hebden, a mining settlement, but it did have for a longish period its own very personal industry - namely, besom making! In the main, local people were employed in agriculture. At Threshfield was the terminus of the Yorkshire Dales Railway, completed in 1901 and now closed. Although the station site has been transformed by modern housing, a railway bridge can still be seen crossing the Burnsall road a short distance out of the village.

Old Threshfield begins where the road from Burnsall meets the Skipton road. Here is the **Park** - what remains of the village green, triangular in shape, with stocks, and sheltered by trees. The old houses and barns are mainly clustered around this green. If we bear left towards the Burnsall road, we see on our left a row of cottages divided by a cul-de-sac, and at the far end of these cottages is **Park Grange,** a fine seventeenth-century building, with mullioned windows and a datestone inscribed F 1640 H.

Turning up the cul-de-sac and continuing on to the end we reach, on the right, **Toft House**, which has, on the road side, a broad gable. The original mullioned windows have been replaced by modern ones at the front but still exist at the back, despite other alterations.

Our route now takes us back to the village green and continues on its left-hand side, passing the old post office and its neighbour which bears a datestone W 1651 H. The next building of note is the **Manor House**: of the original seventeenth-century house only the porch now remains; but this is impressive, with three storeys, containing, on the first floor, a six-light transomed window and, on the second floor, a beautiful rose window. In the gable is a small semicircular window, and the rest of the building has Victorian sash windows. Beyond the Manor House is an interesting shippon with three fine doorways in the gable, over one of which is the date 1661 and over another the initials MH.

Continuing down the road, we come to the stone **bridge** that crosses Threshfield Beck, with an old ford alongside. The most notable feature of the bridge is the massive stones that top the parapets: of a semicircular shape, and containing vertical grooves, these are six feet or more in length. Similar stones can be seen on several old bridges in the area, and probably were quarried on Thorpe Fell.

Across the bridge, on the left, is **Ling House**, famous for being for centuries the home of the Ibbotson family, the celebrated besom makers of Threshfield. This industry was begun by a former mosstrooper and cattle raider of the time of James I, and the whole family continued the trade until the last of the Threshfield besom makers died in 1926. The present Ling House is a modern building on the site of a seventeeth-century structure which had burnt down. There is an attractive cobbled pavement in front of the house, and on the adjoining barn are hung a remarkable variety of shoes - shoes for horses, for pack ponies and for cows.

We now return up the main road, noting, on the left, opposite the Manor House, the ancient pinfold or pound (for straying cattle). Finally, again on the left and facing the green, we reach the **Old Hall Inn,** a late eighteenth-century building with nineteenth century windows at the front and the original Georgian windows at the back. The inn replaces the original **Old Hall,** part of which, possibly a fourteenth- or fifteenth-century structure, with two unusual mullioned windows, forms one of the outbuildings in the yard behind the inn. The Old Hall is possibly the oldest existing domestic building in Upper Wharfedale, older even than the oldest part of Grassington Old Hall.

Having completed this tour of old Threshfield, the visitor should now regain the car, and then drive for a short way up the main road towards Kettlewell, turning off left just past the first petrol station up a side lane leading to **Skyrethorns**. This is a tiny but very picturesque hamlet consisting of a small group of old farmhouses with a miniature green and a stream. We turn sharp right past the houses, up a road labelled 'unsuitable for motor vehicles' (though metalled as far as our route takes us). At a distance of just over a mile

THRESHFIELD. VILLAGE.

MASTILES LANE.
NEIL WINGATE

beyond Skyrethorns, a track can be seen on the left leading to **Calf Hole Cave** (or Heights Cave), the entrance of which is divided into two openings by a natural buttress of limestone. Inside the cave, relics of man from the Iron Age and earlier have been discovered, including some Stone Age tools.

In less than a mile we reach the end of the metalled road, where there are two gates. The car should be parked here, for this is the start of a short round walk. Passing through the left-hand gate and keeping by the wall on the right, in a very short distance **Bordley Stone Circle** is reached. Although much depleted, having been robbed of all but three large stones, these still stand prominently on a 50-foot-diameter bank, and the circle dates from the Middle Bronze Age (1600–1000 BC). It used to be known as 'Druids' Altar'; and indeed even such an incomplete circle as this looks surprisingly dramatic in its setting in the middle of a vast, wild and lonely moorland.

The visitor should now return to the gate, and then go through the other gate at the end of the metalled road, to follow the green track which leads for about a mile, in a roughly north-westerly direction, to join **Mastiles Lane**: a broad, walled green road which rolls gently over the moors from Kilnsey in the east to Malham Tarn in the west. It forms part of the ancient monastic road from Fountains Abbey, through its Malham Moor estates, to the Lake District. Incongruous though it may seem in this immensely peaceful stretch of country, for four centuries (from the mid-twelfth century to the Dissolution of the Monasteries) a constant stream of monastic tenants and officials made this a very busy thoroughfare, driving flocks of sheep, cattle and trains of pack ponies and horses. Fountains Abbey owned vast estates in this area, including Malham Moor as far as Kilnsey and nearly the whole of Littondale, and the moors around us here were one immense sheep walk for the monks' flocks. Originally Mastiles Lane was unwalled, and in some places the route was marked by wayside crosses, the bases of some of which are still visible (though not along the stretch we shall now walk).

Turning left, we walk towards Malham Tarn for less than a mile. Here is some of the finest limestone upland scenery in England, and the feeling of space and freedom is exhilarating. Avoiding the first footpath on the left, we turn left along the second broader track which leads us in about a mile to **Bordley**, properly called Bordley Town. Kilnsey was the grange for the whole of the Fountains Abbey estates in Craven, and Bordley was created as a subgrange, responsible to Kilnsey. Stewards for the Abbey lived here, and south of the present hamlet was a central area of good meadowland, surrounded by sheepfolds and enclosures.

(**Bordley Hall**, which we shall not pass on this walk, is further down the Bordley Beck valley, and was rebuilt in 1749 on the site of an older hall.)

Passing through the hamlet, we now take the track up the hill, avoiding the path leading off to the right along the hillside, until we rejoin the green track we first took from the car on our way to Mastiles Lane. If we now turn right along this footpath, we retrace our steps back to the gate, and return to Grassington via Skyrethorns and Threshfield.

6 HEBDEN & YARNBURY

Walk: allow 4 hours

Grassington's other neighbour in the ancient parish of Linton - Hebden - is visited on this walk, which includes an excellent view not only of the interesting remains of Grassington and Hebden's recent industrial past but also part of a settlement of many centuries' antiquity.

The walk begins at Grassington Town Hall. Turning right along Low Lane (the best place to see Grassington's fascinating roofscape), within 50 yards we branch left into High Lane, the walled green track. Just before we reach the first hawthorn tree on the left, we pass through a stile by a field gate and take the footpath that heads off diagonally upwards across the fields to join Edge Lane, another walled track, where we now turn right. From Edge Lane we obtain a magnificent view across Wharfedale to Thorpe Fell, and it is here that we see to good advantage not only the line of reef knolls which show up as strange light green hillocks contrasting with the darker green of Thorpe and Cracoe Fells behind them, but also the lynchets on the lower slopes between Thorpe and Linton. The reef knolls are still a subject of speculation by geologists, but were probably produced in a similar way to the coral reefs (see p. 50); the lynchets in Thorpe West Field are medieval ploughing terraces. As we reach the open moorland, we see a glorious view of the Vale of Burnsall below with the distinctive Millstone Grit formation of Simon's Seat and its summit

HEBDEN GILL
NEIL WINGATE.

crag at the back.

At the point at which the path forks, we should keep to the wall side and at Pickering End Farm go through the gate to follow the diagonal footpath into the village of Hebden. To see the main part of the village, we should cross the main road and explore the roads opposite.

HEBDEN. Before the coming of the leadmining industry, Hebden was situated on both sides of Hebden Beck behind the Clarendon Hotel. As lead miners and textile workers began to flock to the area, the village expanded further down Hebden Gill, where the houses are now concentrated. Its name is probably derived from *heb* (high) plus *den* (dene, valley), describing its position overlooking the gorge which journeys from the peat moors separating Wharfedale from Nidderdale, through the leadmining country, down to the Wharfe. The oldest cottages, set by the beckside above the main road, are of seventeenth-century origin.

The present road bridge was built in 1827 to replace the old stone bridge higher up the beck which - of an early date, and consequently very narrow - formerly carried the first Grassington to Pateley Bridge turnpike.

The **church**, dedicated to St Peter, and a chapel-of-ease to Linton, was built in 1841 in the Early English style. An old relic of Norse days is the **Thruskell Well** (or Thursgill Well), dedicated to the pagan god Thor. A pagan altar is believed to have existed close to this spot up to a century ago. Although there is another 'Thor's Well' at Burnsall, it is extremely rare for wells to retain their pagan dedications; for example, the other previously pagan wells situated near Burnsall were not only Christianized - as was Thruskell - but were rededicated to Christian saints (St Margaret and St Helen).

Near the village school, built in 1875, is a footpath that leads down to the beck and the old mill dams, rejoining the road at **Hebden Mill**, now cottages, but formerly a cotton mill providing local work after the closure of the lead mines; it was itself closed in 1937. The part of Hebden Gill below the road bridge is very attractive, particularly with the presence of the mill dams.

The chief event in Hebden now is the annual sports day held on August Bank Holiday Monday.

If we now return to the road bridge and recross the main road, we should now take the narrow gated road on the left bank of the beck which leads to a footpath up **Hebden Gill** and on to the moors. After passing through the second gate, we should go through the field gate on the right-hand side. The splendid waterfall, **Scala Force,** is a short walk away. The name suggests the former presence of Norse settlements in the vicinity (Norse *skali* meaning outlying farm).

Returning to the main lane and continuing along it as far as Hole Bottom Farm (Jerry and Ben's), we now take the footpath - a rough mining track leading up through the ruins of Hebden Moor mines (disused mines, shafts and levels) - along the side of Hebden Beck. The scenery here is very wild and rugged, with the beck rushing through the narrow gorge, the sides of which are pitted with the relics of Hebden's industrial past. In about a mile beyond Hole Bottom Farm a broad track leads at a tangent up the hillside and winds its way up the moor to join the Duke's New Road to Yarnbury, a road built under the direction of the Duke of

YARNBURY.
NEIL WINGATE .

Devonshire to link the Yarnbury mines more directly with the Cupola smelt mill. Along this track are situated the main group of the Yarnbury mines, and great care should be taken to avoid disused shafts and drainage tunnels, which can prove dangerous if one strays from the main footpath.

YARNBURY was the administrative centre of the Grassington Moor mining field. Set back from the road on the left, in a clump of trees, are a large detached house - the residence and office of the mining manager - and the cottages of junior mining officials. Beyond these and behind the trees a blacksmith had his workshop and stores. In the roadside opposite is an arched entrance dated 1827 to an incline level - a slanting tunnel leading to deeper mines. At this point the most prominent landmark is the Grassington Moor **Cupola smelt mill chimney**. Another important feature is the dam just above the track from Hebden Gill; this was fed by the Duke's Watercourse, a canal built for the Duke of Devonshire to bring water from Blea Beck Dams, travelling for over six miles around the moors through the whole Grassington mining field. The landscape here is marked by the remains of old shafts and spoil heaps; otherwise it is difficult to envisage this lonely spot as such a vital centre of industry. (For further information about the leadmining industry, see Chapter 3.)

Slightly higher up from Yarnbury, a walled track leads off left for about a mile to the abandoned farmhouse of **Barras** (marked on maps as Bare House). The left-hand branch should be taken where the track forks just before Barras. Passing through the gate to reach the front of the building, we see here a good example of a traditional Dales long house, with the dwelling (on the left) and shippon (on the right) both under one roof. The name means 'hill farm' (from Norse *bargh-hus*), and it is in a characteristic position for a sheep farm of Norse foundation, on the fell edge above Wharfedale; a superb panorama of the surrounding fells is gained at this point. The Norse farm was probably used as a sheep farm by the monks of Fountains Abbey, and, a couple of generations after the sitting tenants had been allowed to buy the property upon the Dissolution of the Monasteries, enough money would have been made in the wool trade for them to rebuild the farm in 1620. Around the farmhouse are walled sheep crofts and a larger enclosure.

From Barras a footpath leads down the fields of High Close into Grassington, passing on the left the most impressive example of a **'Celtic field system'** in the Dales, which covers an area of nearly 300 acres. Despite some modification by medieval ploughing, the site can still be seen clearly as a network of stone and turf banks, enclosing rectangular fields of varying sizes. It was a Romano-British development of agriculture based on arable fields, and was probably associated with the Iron Age settlement on Lea Green (see p. 40).

Just outside Grassington, the footpath joins a walled lane which brings us out into Chapel Street; by turning left, we arrive back at the Town Hall.

7 GRASS WOOD & LEA GREEN

Walk: allow 3 hours

Grassington is particularly fortunate in having on its doorstep not only two equally lovely and entirely different tracts of woodland - one a nature reserve - but also one of the most extensive Iron Age settlements in the country. Taking in, too, a beautiful riverside walk with a fine stretch of rapids, this excursion cannot be followed as a distinct route, since the points of interest are widely scattered, but, with the help of a map, the visitor should easily be able to find his way round this not too vast or lonely area.

It is best to begin at Grassington Bridge (see p. 17), taking the footpath that leads off on the right-hand side on the Grassington bank of the river. The track is easy to follow, passing through a number of stiles and over a little footbridge on its way to join the Conistone road. The view of the valley from **Braithgill** is a superb vista of river and woodland scenery. In about half a mile from the bridge we reach **Ghaistrill's Strid**, a narrow, rocky and wooded gorge which resembles in miniature the Strid in Bolton Woods (see p. 61). Here the Wharfe varies in width as it rushes over a series of white limestone terraces, where cavities in the bedrock have created deep pools. Above Ghaistrill's the scenery is just as delightful, with splendid views both up and down the valley. We shortly enter the first stretch of woodland (Low Wood) which, with its glimpses of the shining river through the trees, is a particularly exquisite sight in autumn.

After emerging on to the Grassington–Conistone road, we walk for a short distance to the left before entering **Grass Wood** on the right-hand side. Extending for over 260 acres from the riverside to the heights of Bastow Wood, Grass Wood is one of the most famous nature reserves in the north of England. The wood covers a rocky limestone scar (terraces of which break through the trees), yielding an exceptional abundance - over 300 varieties - of lovely and rare limestone flora. It is also very rich in archaeological remains: apart from general evidence of old enclosures and settlements, including the remains of circular dwellings of Iron Age people, there is also a ruined Brigantian hill fort in the south-east, **Fort Gregory**. Perched high on a limestone hill - Gregory Scar - this fort, with its massive stone walls, was built by the Brigantes both as a lookout for the Roman advance through Wharfedale and as a refuge for the local population. Here too is evidence of early leadmining.

The pathways have been well planned, and the labyrinth of trees and undergrowth opens out frequently into small clearings and glades with outstanding views of Wharfedale, in particular from the natural limestone terrace of Dewbottom Scar in the centre of the wood. For generations Grass Wood has been used by Grassington people both for recreation and for collection of 'estovers' - brushwood for fuel and herbs for cooking. It is, however, strictly illegal for anyone to pick the wild flowers, since many are of great rarity. It was here too that the Grassington blacksmith Tom Lee lay in wait for Dr Petty and murdered him on his way back home after a quarrel at Kilnsey in 1766 (see p. 14).

At the edges of Grass Wood, some coniferous trees have been planted in recent years, but in the centre the original forest still exists, as it does throughout **Bastow Wood**, which is separated only by a wall from Grass Wood. A path on the north-west side of the latter winds its way through dense forest before entering Bastow Wood through a stile. More natural and primeval in the nature of its woodland growth than Grass Wood, it is mostly wild and unplanted, with numerous clearings and small sections of limestone pavements, in the crevices of which grow a profusion of varied shrubs and uncommon plants. Since the trees and flora are all native, we gain a good impression of the appearance of the Wharfedale fell ridges ages ago, before the ancient forests were cleared and eroded. The most recent noticeable alteration in Bastow Wood is an eighteenth-century one: a number of walled, grassy enclosures were created by lead miners for pasturing the ponies and donkeys used in the mines.

Higher up the fellside, above Bastow Wood, lies **Lea Green**, famous for the impressive remains of its **Iron Age settlement**, one of the largest in the country, extending over some 300 acres of limestone pasture. The evidence of this village, which was occupied from around 200 BC to the fifth century AD, is in the form of numerous rectangular field areas enclosed by grassy ridges, with a few hut circles scattered among them, and fragments of a road system. An Iron Age population occupied most of the Pennines and carried on the clearance of the woodland, particularly on the limestone terraces, domesticating and breeding sheep and cattle. Since it would have been completely invisible from the Roman legions in the villages below, the settlement would also have formed an ideal retreat for the small, rebellious tribe of Brigantes. Human and other remains which have been excavated here - including relics in flint, bone, stone, iron and bronze - all point to the site's having been continuously inhabited throughout the Roman occupation, although no trace of actual Roman construction has been found. The 'Celtic field system' on High Close (see p. 38) would probably have been associated with this site on Lea Green.

After these early days, the Angles from the new village of Grassington below grazed their animals here, and a large dew pond, probably dating from Brigantian times, is still in use. Apart from the evidence of ancient settlement, an even earlier relic can be seen on Lea Green, a large **Bronze Age barrow** of around 1600 BC, which was probably used later (as a meeting place?) by the Iron Age population. Returning to rather more recent times, the rows of circular holes and connecting trenches are the remains of fifteenth-century leadmining.

A track leads south-east across Lea Green to join the paths from Bastow and Grass Woods, eventually to end at Town Head Farm in Grassington. After we have left the rough, open ground of Lea Green, and entered the grassy farm fields, even clearer indications of the Iron Age settlement can be seen. Just before we reach a steep slope with a narrow stile at the top, there is a field with a deep hollow, across which the ground is distinctly marked by the rectangular areas earlier described. Reaching Town Head Farm (see p. 14), we turn left along Chapel Street and re-enter the centre of Grassington.

8 ROUND CONISTONE

Car trip plus walk: allow 2½ hours

After driving to Conistone along the back road on the right-hand side of the Wharfe, a short round walk takes in some of the most impressive and characteristic limestone scenery in Wharfedale, as well as allowing the visitor the opportunity to see yet another of Wharfedale's harmonious villages.

The route begins at Wood Lane, from where a winding narrow road leads to Conistone, where the car should be parked. On arriving here, one can immediately see that the hills have already become more majestic, and that the Great Scar Limestone of Craven is more prominent here than further down the dale. One's first impression is one of harmony: fields, hills, drystone walls, crags and cottages all blend in together, particularly since all the building here is in local stone. The striking bridge that links Conistone with Kilnsey was first built in monastic times, as part of the route from Fountains Abbey to the Lake District via Mastiles Lane (see p. 33) and Malham Moor.

The name is probably Anglian for 'king's enclosure': in support of this theory, in the Domesday Book Conistone is included among lands held by the king's thanes. Whatever the meaning of its name, Conistone is a perfect example of an Anglian settlement, with its green around which all the houses are grouped, its meadowland on the valley floor, the strips of arable land with lynchets (ploughing terraces) on the rising ground up to the foot of the first limestone scars, and the common pastures above the scars rising from 1000 to 1500 feet, with the moorland beyond.

Until the formation of the parish council of Conistone-with-Kilnsey, local government since 1583 had been almost entirely by the 'bylawmen', representatives of the inhabitants and freeholders acting as lords of the manor, controlling the grazing rights and appointing a barmaster to regulate the lead mines on Conistone Moor and at Mossdale in the seventeenth century. (Compare the Trust Lords at Kettlewell, p. 63.)

In the Enclosure Award of 1793 Conistone and Kettlewell were granted the right to enclose 8000 acres of commons and pastures. Conistone Old Pasture had already been enclosed in the twelfth century to keep stock from wandering over the wasteland; and the 'New Close' was enclosed in 1587 to improve the poor common pasture by regulating the grazing. Thus the different stages of enclosure walling can clearly be seen, the older walls curving and irregular, and the later ones of the Enclosure Act of 1801 climbing the hillside in straight lines because they were planned on paper.

In this compact village, the oldest houses are seventeenth century, and many have interesting door heads: there is one datestone inscribed RC 1657, another IT 1697 and a third 1705. And despite its slight leadmining history, the village's atmosphere is indisputably rural.

At the back of the village is a remarkable dry limestone gorge, **Gurling Trough** (known also as 'The Gorge', 'The Gill' or 'The Dib'). A footpath leads through a gate into this ravine, which at first sight looks quite impassable, yet which can easily be negotiated, despite the fact that the dry river

GURLING TROUGH.

bed is a mass of huge boulders. Following the rough track, we emerge to a surprise view of a dry green valley, soft, rolling and immensely peaceful, with limestone outcrops

LIMESTONE PAVEMENT.

NEIL WINGATE.

decorating the slopes. Where a path branches off to the right up a side valley, we take the left fork which climbs steeply up the hillside to join Scot Gate, a broad track from Conistone to Mossdale, where formerly there were lead mines.

The scar above us to the left is Hill Castle Scar, and if we bear right up Scot Gate we climb above the scar to get a magnificent view of a **limestone pavement**. A characteristic feature of the Great Scar Limestone scenery, this has been formed by the dissolving of the limestone by rainwater, which has carved the exposed rock into an intricate pattern of deep channels along joints (or 'grikes') separating blocks of remaining limestone ('clints'). In the grikes is a rich variety of ferns and many former woodland plants - evidence of the time before the clearance of the forest by early man and his grazing animals. The pavement's extraordinary appearance is enhanced by the crooked trees growing between the clints. For anyone who has never seen a large limestone pavement before, this particular one is a most spectacular sight.

If we face towards Wharfedale, on our right, some short distance away is a particularly fine example of a **field kiln**. Such limekilns, built of limestone, are almost as common a feature of the Wharfedale landscape as the drystone walls. Most belong to the eighteenth or nineteenth century and have in the main been disused for more than a century. They were used by farmers to burn limestone for the purpose of producing lime to spread on the land as a manure and to reduce the acidity of the soil. Like this particular example, the kiln was usually built near a small scar from which the limestone supply could easily be carried.

This walk is made even more rewarding by the beauty of the surrounding scenery. From here we have a breathtaking panorama over Wharfedale, taking in Great Whernside, the hill shoulder between Wharfedale and Littondale, Malham Moor with Kilnsey Crag and Mastiles Lane clearly visible, as well as Thorpe Fell and Barras (see p. 38) perched on the edge of the moor. This part of Conistone pasture is still very largely open sheep walk, consisting of a series of terraces and scarps up the fells - difficult terrain for the shepherd.

The walk back down Scot Gate is to be savoured slowly, for the view is consistently enchanting, all the way back down to the Conistone road - notably, the fascinating shapes of Gurling Trough as seen from above, and the sight of Littondale and Upper Wharfedale in the same prospect.

Turning left at the bottom of the track, in a few yards **Conistone Church** is reached, dedicated to St Mary, and claimed to be of Saxon foundation and thus the oldest church in Wharfedale. However, the Norman church that followed was almost entirely rebuilt, albeit in Norman style, in 1846. On the north side of the nave, two massive Norman arches remain, and a two-light window with triangular heads, now in the vestry, is probably of the same date. There are two Perpendicular arches on the east side of the nave. The porch, again in Norman style, is modern. Until 1876 the church was part of the parish of Burnsall; it then became a chapel-of-ease to Rylstone; and it now forms part of the parish of Kettlewell.

The walk terminates at Conistone village.

9 BURNSALL & THORPE

Walk: allow 4½ hours
This route includes a delightful riverside walk along the Wharfe, and visits to one of the most attractive villages in the dale as well as to one of the most mysterious.

The walk begins at Grassington Bridge (see p. 17), where we take the riverside path which leads off to the left on the Grassington side of the river, passing Low Mill (see p. 22), Isingdale Beck and the lovely Lythe Wood before reaching the **Swing Bridge** (suspension bridge) near Hebden, which takes our route across to the other side of the Wharfe. At first the path keeps close to the edge of the river, passing two ancient wells, dedicated to St Helen and St Margaret; these were probably originally dedicated to pagan gods, being later Christianized and given saints' names. Such well worship continued as a curious survival of paganism until the nineteenth century. Very soon we reach the impressive **Loup Scar,** where the Wharfe surges over huge boulders through overhanging limestone cliffs. This dramatic gorge is the place where, as tradition has it, the Grassington murderer Tom Lee threw the body of his victim, Dr Petty, into the river. For a short way the path climbs over the top of the scars, reaching the river level again near Burnsall.

BURNSALL. This very pretty village lies in the rolling country where the Wharfedale landscape begins to change from the distinctive limestone uplands to the softer scenery and gritstone moorlands characteristic of this lower stretch

BURNSALL CHURCH AND GRAMMAR SCHOOL

of the dale. Here we are in Viking country: Burnsall itself was probably named after some Norse chieftain (Brun? Bjorn? plus Danish *sal*, hall); and the many ancient remains to be found in and around the church suggest that the village is of very old foundation, and that the ancient Norse and Anglo-Danish cultures persisted here for some time. However, Burnsall has the appearance of a typical Dales village, with its mellow seventeenth-century houses with mullioned windows, its green and its two inns - the Red Lion and the Fell Hotel. Burnsall Sports have been an annual event since the time of Elizabeth I, held on the green in August. The sports include a fell race which is the oldest of its kind in the country, having been inaugurated around 1850.

It is very much a linear village in formation, and at the top of the street on the right is the fine **Church**. Although it was largely rebuilt in the reign of Henry VIII, and little remains in the present structure that is earlier than Perpendicular, it is almost certain that before the original Norman church was built there was something more than a preaching cross at Burnsall. Evidence that the church had been founded long before - possibly as early as the ninth or tenth century - is demonstrated by the font and the ancient relics inside the church. During the restoration of 1859 several **Anglo-Danish crosses** were found built into the walls and were removed. Now twelve fragments of these crosses can be seen inside the church, as well as two **hog-back tombstones** of the tenth century modelled like the typical Norse or Danish long house. The **font**, though Norman, bears crude carvings on the base and at the foot of the bowl which are in the Norse tradition. Also discovered during the restoration was a fine sculptured **alabaster panel** of the fourteenth or fifteenth century, depicting the Adoration of the Magi, and still displaying some of its original colour and gilding. The oldest part of the church, however, is the two windows of around 1300 at the east end of the south chancel chapel; the stained glass here, though, is modern. There is also a handsome Jacobean pulpit. Old stocks can be seen in a corner of the churchyard, which is entered by a seventeenth-century lychgate, operated by a system of weights.

A tablet in the south aisle of the church commemorates the work of Sir William Craven who in 1612 repaired and 'butified' the church at his own expense, as well as repairing several bridges and building the **Grammar School**. This schoolhouse, just below the church, was founded by Sir William Craven in 1602. Craven, known as the 'Dick Whittington of the Dales', was born in Appletreewick and went to London where he found fame and fortune, eventually becoming Lord Mayor in 1610–11. The school was endowed as a free grammar school for boys of the parish, and boarding was provided: the upper storey was divided into dormitory chambers by oak panelling, a structure that still exists today. Although it continued as a grammar school until 1876, by that time a small fee was being charged; but it is still in use, as a state primary school. The building resembles a small manor house, and is a magnificent example of the domestic architecture of that age. The two-storeyed gabled porch and the beautiful mullioned windows with their heavily leaded lights are particularly striking.

Returning back down the street we reach the **Red Lion**,

BURNSALL BRIDGE AND RED LION.

named after the arms of the Hartlington family. Despite much enlargement, this long, low building with mullioned windows still retains the character of a Dales inn.

Burnsall Bridge is a lovely old stone bridge of five arches. Although it was built as recently as 1884, to replace one built in 1827 and destroyed in a flood, the present structure apparently retains the features of the one built by Sir William Craven in 1612 - 'over the Wherfe att Burnsall, a very fair one' - which itself replaced another that had been destroyed in a flood. But despite this succession of floods and rebuilding, Burnsall's existing bridge still dominates the village when seen from a distance.

We now retrace our steps as far as the sharp right-angled bend in the road, where we take a footpath that begins at an old farmhouse on the corner at the left-hand side. This extremely pleasant walk takes us through narrow fields and a succession of stiles, running parallel to the road at first and crossing over three narrow lanes, before heading directly for the right-hand side of Kail Hill. Passing by the left corner of Skulbert's Wood, the footpath leads into Kail Lane and so into Thorpe.

THORPE. Lying in a deep hollow between Kail Hill in the east and Elbolton in the west, Thorpe-sub-montem (or Thorpe-in-the-Hollow) well deserves its nickname, 'the hidden village', for it is not visible from any point in the valley. Since the visitor does not see the village until he is actually entering it, the first view of the place is astonishing, and the village quite unique in Wharfedale in this respect. Its name, meaning 'outlying hamlet', is Danish in origin, but Thorpe's history goes back to prehistoric times.

The hills that conceal Thorpe so perfectly are the 1660-foot gritstone Thorpe Fell behind and the two rounded hills of Kail and Elbolton. The two latter hills are part of Wharfedale's strange phenomenon known as the **reef knolls**: peculiar bright green hills contrasting strongly with the dark grit of Thorpe and Cracoe Fells behind them. Although still the subject of speculation, it is believed that these were formed similarly to the coral reefs; in composition they are mounds of limestone, rich in fossil corals and shells, and with veins of lead running through them. Their names are well suited to such mysterious formations: Kail, Elbolton, Stebden, Langerton (below the road and a long, low hill), Butterhaw, Carden and Skelterton (with a clump of trees on the summit).

These hills kept the secret of Thorpe so closely that, it is said, during the period of the frequent Scottish raids of the fourteenth and fifteenth centuries, the Scots never discovered this place, which consequently became a refuge for Dalespeople.

But it is inside **Elbolton** itself that Thorpe's most astounding secret was found. Within this hill is contained a prehistoric cave known as **Navvy Noddle Hole** (or Knave Knoll Hole), and here were discovered not only human remains that suggest the cave was used both as an occasional dwelling and as a burial place between 2000 and 3000 years ago, but also, at a lower level, the remains of Arctic animals such as reindeer and bears which must have occupied the cave at the end of the Ice Age. A more recent sight on Elbolton is the evidence of leadmining - lines of bell pits of the fifteenth and sixteenth centuries as well as later shafts.

A legend of comparatively modern growth, with apparently no foundation in contemporary documents, is that Thorpe was a village of shoemakers. Pontefract and Hartley state that at one time there were forty cobblers living here and that as late as 1822 there were two shoemakers and one bootmaker. Even Harry Speight, writing in 1900, says that in earlier days Thorpe-made boots and shoes were famous for their quality for miles around. But we must accept that this popular story, however attractive, is no more than myth.

Returning to a more evident reality, we can see in Thorpe a tiny, tree-sheltered green, round which are gathered some very substantially built houses with mullioned windows and stone lintels, some of which have now been converted into barns and shippons. There is even a **Manor House**, an excellent Georgian building with an oak staircase and a fine oak-panelled room inside. Thorpe Fell Lane leads to the common pastures and the old peat pits on Thorpe Fell, and a green road turning slightly to the right near the top of the street takes one on to the flanks of Elbolton.

To return to Grassington, we bear right out of the village, shortly taking the right-hand fork to join the Burnsall–Threshfield main road, and in a short distance a footpath on the right heads off diagonally across the fields, bearing round Stickhaw Hill to join the Linton Church road halfway between Linton Mill and the church by a house at the end of a lane. Going left along the church road, and turning right to cross the Tin Bridge over Linton Falls (see p. 21), we continue up the Snake Walk to the Hebden road which returns us to the foot of Grassington Main Street.

10 DOWNDALE TO BOLTON ABBEY

Car tour: allow 4 hours
Further down Wharfedale the scenery changes from limestone uplands to soft, rolling country and dark gritstone moorlands. Our route passes through the ancient Forest of Barden, the tract of land reserved in Norman times for hunting, which had its own laws for the preservation of wild animals; and includes an ancient and picturesque tower, the most beautifully situated monastic ruin in England, lovely old bridges, a pretty stone-built village with three halls, and a fascinating specimen of industrial archaeology.

Bearing left beyond Grassington Bridge along the road to Burnsall (see p. 46), we take the right-hand fork past the Fell Hotel and continue through the coniferous forest along the road which runs high above the Wharfe, overlooking Appletreewick and Simon's Seat.

We soon reach the majestic ruin of **Barden Tower,** built by Lord Henry Clifford in 1485 and beautifully restored in 1658–9 by Lady Anne Clifford. Originally this was the chief of the Cliffords' six hunting lodges in the Forest of Barden. Lord Henry Clifford had been a refugee from the Wars of the Roses, and it is traditionally believed that from boyhood he had lived with shepherds until his titles and estates were restored to him in 1485 by Henry VIII. However, since he had apparently become accustomed to the simple life (being known as the 'Shepherd Lord'), he chose rather than Skipton Castle the seclusion of the Forest Lodge as his chief

home, where he studied with the canons of Bolton Priory; but it is doubtful that he was the recluse of popular tradition, since he did some entertaining there and also spent some time at Skipton. In 1513 he left to lead a troop of Dalesmen to victory at Flodden Field, and after his death in 1523 the tower decayed until its restoration in 1658–9. It again fell into disprepair, in the late eighteenth century the roof was removed and it became a ruin. However, it remains an impressive tower house of three storeys, subdivided into apartments with great fireplaces in many of the rooms.

Across a yard from the tower is **Chapel House**. The chapel - a private one for Barden Tower until after the Reformation, when it became a chapel-of-ease to Bolton - and its adjoining farmhouse form an interesting seventeenth-century construction, with tall mullioned windows and a tower with a porch beneath. (Near Barden Tower too is the well-known Yorkshire Crafts Shop.)

It is well worthwhile driving down the side road on the left to see **Barden Bridge**, one of the loveliest in the dale, stone-built in 1659 and 'repayred at the charge of the whole West Riding' in 1676 (as the inscription on the north parapet reads). Beyond its three graceful arches is a glorious view down the dale, and its stones bear many mason marks. Like other Wharfedale bridges, it suffered damage in successive floods and was extensively repaired in 1955.

Returning to the main road, we now drive along a beautiful stretch of the Wharfe, with Bolton Woods below us. Here is the **Strid**, a narrow gorge where many people have been killed attempting to leap across; although it is only a few feet wide, the bank is so formed that on landing one can easily lose one's balance and slip backwards into the 30-foot depths and strong currents. The most famous of the Strid's victims was the 'Boy of Egremond', the son of Alice de Romille who granted the Augustinian canons their land at Bolton; he was returning from the hunt with his greyhound on a lead, jumped over the Strid, but the dog dragged him back and he was drowned. There is no truth in the story that this occasioned the founding of Bolton Priory by his mother, since his name appears on the foundation deeds; and even the manner of the boy's death may be pure legend.

There is an interesting Nature Trail through Strid Wood (see Chapter 11), reached from either the Strid Car Park or the **Cavendish Pavilion** (refreshments), where too a bridge gives access to the opposite bank. We reach the Pavilion by turning off left at the **Cavendish Memorial**, a hexagonal, neo-Gothic fountain built in 1886 to the memory of Lord Frederick Cavendish, the son of the seventh Duke of Devonshire. It is possible to take in one of the Strid Wood walks on this trip, though the Nature Trail can be better explored if it is made a separate excursion.

Just past the Cavendish Memorial is **Bolton Priory**. With its unique background of meadows, woodland, moorland and mountain - a perfect blend of the soft and gentle with the rugged and wild - Bolton Priory has been a favourite sketching ground of many artists, including Turner. Although it is usually called Bolton Abbey, it was in fact a priory, first endowed in 1120 at Embsay by Cecily de Romille and her husband William Meschines for Augustinian canons. In 1154 the founders' daughter, Alice de Romille, granted them their present site at Bolton. Building began almost immediately with the church, the earliest part surviving only as ruins (at the west end of the ruined chancel). By 1220 the church, chapter house and the domestic buildings were almost complete, and benefactors soon provided the priory with extensive lands and property, including farms, mines and granges. A grand rebuilding and extension scheme was begun in the fourteenth century, which included the chapter house, gatehouse and other domestic buildings. In 1520 Prior Moone began work on the West Tower, but this remained unfinished; for, with the Dissolution of the Monasteries, a deed of surrender was signed in 1539. The nave of the priory church, however, was allowed to remain in use. The Bolton lands mainly reverted to their patrons, the Cliffords, Bolton Abbey becoming eventually part of the Duke of Devonshire's estate.

Access to the priory is either by the drive near the archway over the road, or through the 'Hole-in-the-Wall' (a gap in the precinct wall) - a good vantage point for seeing the priory ruins in their setting; the hollows on either side of the path were the priory's fishponds.

The most intact part of Bolton Priory is the nave of the original priory church, now preserved as the parish church. It is entered by the thirteenth-century **West Front**, a superb example of Early English architecture, partially obscured, however, by Prior Moone's unfinished and very ornate Perpendicular **West Tower**, commenced in 1520. Inside, the clerestory has four lancet windows, and the Decorated windows of the aisle are fourteenth century. On the south side are six tall two-light windows with plate tracery (*c.* 1240).

The ruined buildings include the rest of the priory church

BOLTON PRIORY
NEIL WINGATE

(the chancel and transepts); on the south side of the nave the cloisters, broken at the north-east corner for a doorway of around 1290; the octangular chapter house (about 1360); the infirmary; the dormitory; the refectory (early thirteenth century); and the prior's lodging (fourteenth century).

On the south side of the ruins is the **Rectory**, constructed from part of the infirmary buildings, originally as a grammar school, called the Boyle School. This eventually became a schoolhouse and parsonage in one; after the school was closed, it was sold in 1874 to the Duke of Devonshire and has since been the rectory. The north-east angle is fifteenth century, and the original six-light window of the infirmary is preserved in the north side here. The rest of the house, with its long mullioned windows, is mainly sixteenth century.

Across the lawns to the west of the priory is **Bolton Hall**, incorporating in its centre the fourteenth-century priory gatehouse - a fine three-storeyed structure with four towers. Extensions were added on either side in the eighteenth century, when the original entrances through the gatehouse were walled up. In 1843 extensive alterations were carried out for the Duke of Devonshire, the present Duke now using Bolton Hall for shooting parties in August.

We cannot leave Bolton Priory without briefly recounting the legend of the 'White Doe of Rylstone', commemorated in a poem by Wordsworth. The Norton family of Rylstone took part in the Rising of the North of 1569, the only survivor being the daughter Emily. Her brother Francis had given her a white doe which became Emily's sole companion on her frequent journeys from Rylstone to Bolton Abbey to weep over her brother's tomb there. It is said that she died of grief, and that the white doe still haunts the priory ruins.

A word about Bolton village, actually much older in foundation than the priory: there is a tithe barn (rebuilt), and the archway over the road was an aqueduct, probably built in the eighteenth century to carry water to a mill built on the site of that of the priory.

Continuing south, we fork left beyond the Devonshire Arms Hotel to take the road which, crossing **Bolton Bridge**, climbs over the moors to Blubberhouses and Harrogate. There was a bridge with a chapel here as early as the fourteenth century, formerly in the care of Bolton Priory. In 1676, after successive destructions of the wooden bridge by floods, the present stone bridge was built; it has since been widened to twice its original size, the older portion being the downstream side.

On the left, about half a mile beyond Bolton Bridge, is **Beamsley Hospital**. Founded in 1593 by Lady Margaret Russell to provide free accommodation for thirteen poor women of Skipton, the almshouses were restored in the seventeenth century by her daughter, Lady Anne Clifford (the restorer of Barden Tower), and seven tenants now occupy seven houses rent free. The main structure consists of a circular chapel from which seven cottages radiate.

In a short distance, a narrow, gated metalled road leads off to the left, signposted to **Storiths** (once a flourishing agricultural outlier to Bolton Priory). From the top of this road (near the summit of Storiths Crag on the right) is the most breathtaking view of Wharfedale from Bolton Abbey upwards. The road then descends steeply to the woods and the unexpected (and entertaining) ford over Pickles Beck.

VIEW FROM STORITHS

NEIL WINGATE.

CRAVEN ARMS AND STOCKS, APPLETREEWICK. NEIL WINGATE.

We continue up the east side of Wharfedale, past the Valley of Desolation on the right, and, as the valley widens out after the Strid, we approach the village of APPLETREEWICK, known by locals as 'Aptrick', and meaning 'the village near an apple tree' (*wick* is Norse for village). Although of old foundation, Appletreewick's growth dates from monastic times, when in 1300 the ancient manor passed to the canons of Bolton Priory. With its sheep ranges and lead mines, Appletreewick was a valuable acquisition, and was a principal grange for 250 years. The benefits were mutual; for under the ownership of the canons the village prospered, and around 1310 a charter was granted for a weekly market and an annual fair lasting four days. The fair was an important event for miles around until the growth of the railways in the mid-nineteenth century. The fame of its onions caused it in latter days to be known as Appletreewick Onion Fair, which name is commemorated in the street called Onion Lane where the onions were hung. The sheep and cattle were grazed in the large pasture above the Craven Arms which is still called Sheep Fair Hill. Stone water troughs down Cork Street were used for watering cattle. Appletreewick was also a centre of leadmining until the nineteenth century, after which its economy suffered badly.

The steep main street with stone-built houses mainly of sixteenth- and seventeenth-century date is an attraction in itself. The first notable building is seen on the left just as we enter the village. **High Hall**, restored by Sir William Craven, is a typical seventeenth-century home of the wealthier yeoman classes, but possessing some features only to be found in the more superior houses. It is a three-storeyed house with a porch formerly of two storeys. Inside, a large banqueting hall has a minstrel's gallery with a carved oak screen. Although it was built mainly in the seventeenth century, the style is Elizabethan. In some of the windows are diamond-paned leaded lights. Now a farmhouse, High Hall was the former home of the Earls of Craven; it is probable that there had been a hall on this site since the Norman Conquest.

Slightly lower down, on the opposite side, is the tiny chapel-of-ease to Burnsall, **St John**. It was converted in 1897–8 from two cottages, in one of which Sir William Craven is reputed to have been born in 1548. Craven was the 'Dick Whittington of the Dales' who went to London as a boy, became Sheriff in 1600–1 and Lord Mayor in 1610c11); he endowed the Grammar School at Burnsall, and repaired Burnsall Church and several bridges, as well as rebuilding High Hall. This neat stone building was restored in 1933 and the woodwork is by Robert Thompson of Kilburn.

Lower down, on the left, is **Monk's Hall** (or Mock Beggar Hall), on the site of Bolton Priory's grange, and largely rebuilt in 1697. Inside the house is some fifteenth-century work. The projecting right wing of the outbuilding has an unusual façade: the door is reached by an outside staircase; the upper windows have lintel stones decorated with semi-eircles; and there are ornate pigeon holes above the windows and over the doorway.

On the right of the road we reach the New Inn, near which is the old pound for straying animals. The other inn, further down on the same side, is the Craven Arms; nearby, at the entrance to a track leading to a network of disused lead mines on the moor as far as Greenhow, stand the old villagc

stocks. Opposite is Onion Lane, leading down to the river.

Just as we are leaving the village we see, on the left, the third imposing building, **Low Hall**. Now a farmhouse, it is of an early date; restored in 1658 and again in 1868, it retains many of its original features. The gabled end has a nine-light transomed window on the ground floor, a six-light transomed window above, and a stepped three-light window in the gable. The original oak door, an oak-panelled entrance hall and an oak staircase remain.

Bearing round the side of Kail Hill, we pass the elegant seventeenth-century yeoman's house, **Woodhouse Manor** (set back from the road), which is all that remains of the former sizeable manor belonging to Bolton Priory.

We now reach Hartlington Bridge, where a track leads off to the right to **Hartlington Mill**, a seventeenth-century building with a superb iron water wheel which until comparatively recently powered the tools of a carpenter's shop. Originally a corn mill, after some repairs it had become a worsted mill; it was last used in the Second World War to generate electricity. As a striking example of Dales industrial archaeology, the mill is well worth seeing.

The house at the bridge, Bridge House, was originally an inn called Spout Yett (or Yat), and was rebuilt in 1882. Hartlington Hall, set back among trees on the right, is a late nineteenth-century building, and Hartlington itself used to exist as an independent manor.

At Hartlington we fork right and then branch off left along the **Skuff road** to Hebden, a delightful route with wonderful views of Burnsall and the river. By turning left along the main road at Hebden, we return to Grassington.

11 STRID WOOD NATURE TRAIL

Six short trails, of varying lengths

The Strid (see p. 53) is a long gorge caused by the erosion of the bedrock into potholes which joined to form a deep, constricted passage through which the river rushes with tremendous force, gaining impetus from the sudden narrowing of the Wharfe and the steep drop at the Strid's entrance. In Strid Wood are several skilfully planned walks, with exquisite prospects of river and woodland, and seats placed at good viewpoints. We owe the existence of these paths to the Rev. William Carr of Bolton Priory Church, who planned about 30 miles of walks in Bolton Woods for the Duke of Devonshire in the nineteenth century, when people came from miles around to experience a wagonette trip and walk to the Strid. The pathways on the west bank have been turned into a series of fascinating nature trails, each one offering different facets of botany, wildlife and geology. They are described fully in the guidebook with map, obtained at the two access points - the Cavendish Pavilion and the Strid Car Park. Among the trees are Norway spruce, Scots pine, larch, sycamore, oak and alder; the birds include the heron, wagtail, sandpiper, dipper and jay. Primroses, wood sorrel, bluebells and meadowsweet bloom here, and the grey squirrel, water vole, rabbits and a variety of insects including the dragonfly and various butterflies are to be seen. Of geological interest are the sulphur well and the South Craven Fault in the limestone crossing the Wharfe.

12 UPDALE TO LANGSTROTHDALE

Car tour: allow 5 hours
Updale from Grassington we enter the landscape of the Great Scar Limestone of Craven, with its limestone crags and high pastures above the valley floor where the ribbon of the Wharfe winds through lush meadows and woodland, finally to reach the wild grandeur of Langstrothdale and the source of the Wharfe.

The route begins at Wood Lane, where we take the back road on the right of the river through Conistone (see p. 42) to Kettlewell, a route that passes Grass Wood (see p. 40) and from which we gain superb views up the dale, with Kilnsey Crag (see p. 70) across the valley dramatically dominating the scene. Shortly before we reach Kettlewell, we pass **Scargill House** on the right, a Church of England holiday and conference centre with a Scandinavian-style church; Scargill is a good vantage point for seeing the formation of the upper dale with its glacier-carved U-shape.

KETTLEWELL. Situated in the mouth of the valley made by the junction of Cam and Dowber Gills, Kettlewell is built on both banks of Cam Beck. Its name is derived from Ketel, a Norse-Irish chieftain into whose possession the village came before the Norman Conquest, but the lynchets (ploughing terraces) on the lower slopes are evidence that this was originally an Anglian settlement. Kettlewell owes its importance, however, to the fact that in the twelfth century part of the manor was granted to the monks of the

Premonstratensian abbey of Coverham; the route over into Coverdale was probably created by the monks. Bolton Priory and Fountains Abbey also had lands here, so that, with its early market (through a thirteenth-century charter) and its monastic connections, it must have been a thriving community. The village was a centre of both textiles and leadmining - the latter being responsible for its growth in the eighteenth and nineteenth centuries, lead having been mined for centuries in the surrounding hills and smelted locally. Many of the fell tracks here owe their origins either to the lead miners or to the monks. Near the confluence of Dowber and Cam Becks are the foundations of the old lead smelt mill, where ore was smelted from neighbouring mines; in use from around 1700 to 1886, it was demolished in 1942. The cotton mill was converted in 1805 from a water-powered corn mill, but was pulled down in 1856.

By the sixteenth century, Coverham Abbey owned one part of Kettlewell manor and the Nevilles of Middleham Castle owned the other part; but following the Dissolution of the Monasteries and the sequestration of the Nevilles' lands after the Rising of the North of 1569, the whole manor passed to the Crown. In 1628 Charles I granted the manor to London merchants who in 1656 sold it to a group of local men. These eventually became the **Trust Lords** of Kettlewell, elected from the freeholders, who kept the manorial rights and dues in trust: to them were paid royalties from the mines and quarries; it was they who regulated the use of the common pasture and the cutting of peat (turbary rights) and bracken. This system still operates today: the Trust Lords draw rent from land in their possession and use the income for improvements in Kettlewell.

There are not many old buildings here that have been left unaltered, most having been rebuilt in the late nineteenth century, but the river bridge is a beautiful old structure that carries a wealth of mason marks on its stones, and a small number of seventeenth- and eighteenth-century houses still remain, including the vicarage. The **Church of St Mary** is a nineteenth-century building constructed to replace the original Norman church which was demolished in 1819; the tower dates from 1820, and the nave and chancel were built between 1882 and 1885. Of the original church only the twelfth- or thirteenth-century circular font remains, with the three boars' heads of the Percy badge.

There are many good walks from Kettlewell: a pretty riverside path to Buckden; a track up Dowber Gill is an approach to Great Whernside (2308 feet); 'Top Mere Road', a green road up the fellside behind Kettlewell, leads over the hills to Waldendale, or joins the motor road to Coverdale, as well as joining 'Starbotton Road' (at Cam Head), a similar green road leading left to Starbotton; a footpath leads over the hill shoulder to Arncliffe in Littondale. There are three inns - the Bluebell Hotel, the King's Head and the Race Horses Hotel.

Bearing left over the bridge towards Buckden, we enter a steep-sided valley where the slopes are patterned with limestone walls running from the meadows on the valley floor to the tops of the fells, decorated with an extraordinary number of isolated **field barns.** These barns, or 'laithes', belong to the era before the tractor when it was easier to sweep hay directly into separate barns where cattle could be accommodated and fed from a near source; they are now little used because the current tendency is towards centrally situated, all-purpose single buildings. The area around Starbotton is the best place to see this very distinctive feature of the Dales landscape (see p. 5).

STARBOTTON. Two miles up the road from Kettlewell, Starbotton is an unspoilt village built on a bed of glacial moraine at the foot of Cam Gill, a narrow and precipitous ravine. Since very little building or restoration was required during the Victorian era, it consists chiefly of houses of the seventeenth to the early nineteenth century, built by local masons in local stone, with mullioned windows and stone-slated roofs, many houses bearing carved doorheads with dated lintels, such as WF 1656, TS 1665, 1664 and the earliest, 1621. These early dates are interesting, because in 1686 the worst Wharfedale flood in recorded history almost completely engulfed Starbotton: many houses were totally destroyed, and none escaped serious damage. With the development of the leadmining industry, some Georgian houses were built, with plain doorways and sash windows. On the back road, near the mouth of the gill, is the old hall or manor house; dated stones from other houses have been built into it, but its own datestone is WS 1663 TS. The village barns generally have projecting wings, an open porch and air slits in the walls for drying corn when this was grown in the dale; in some of the gable ends are decorative pigeon holes, a common feature of Dales barns - a practical one, too, since the pigeons provided the farmers with extra food. The Fox and Hounds inn was almost entirely rebuilt in 1834 in the Georgian style.

The name Starbotton could be Norse, meaning 'settlement at the head of the dale', or else Anglo-Saxon, meaning 'stony valley bottom'; but its origins were probably Anglian. The only remains of its leadmining history are the derelict smelt mill chimney in the mouth of the gill behind the village and the many old tracks to Kettlewell which served the lead miners. There are a number of good walks, including the green road called 'Starbotton Road' leading towards the head of Coverdale (once part of an ancient packhorse trail) and joining at Cam Head the 'Top Mere Road' to Kettlewell, as well as the green track climbing the hill shoulder on the up-dale side of the village (the Knuckle Bone) to the summit of Buckden Pike (2302 feet) and to the disused mines on Buckden Gavel; another clear track climbs over Old Cote Moor to Arncliffe in Littondale. At the lower end of the village, below the road, is the small walled enclosure with tall trees that is a long-disused Quaker burial ground.

We now continue for two miles up the road to Buckden, noting the good examples of Anglian lynchets on the lower slopes. Where the river runs nearest to the road in its biggest bend, just over a hedge on the right can be seen an old cross still standing in its socket. This marks the boundary, not only between the ancient chapelry of Hubberholme and the parish of Kettlewell, but also between the old Norman hunting Forests of Langstrothdale and Litton.

BUCKDEN. Situated just within the boundary of Langstrothdale Chase, Buckden owes its origins and growth to its being chosen as the residence of the Forest officials, probably in the twelfth century. Its very name demonstrates its connections with hunting, meaning 'the valley of the bucks', and up

SCARGILL HOUSE AND VIEW UPDALE.

until well into the twentieth century deer grazed on the hill slopes around Buckden. At the point where three main routes meet, Buckden once boasted three inns and two autumn fairs for sheep and cattle. Outside the sole remaining inn, the Buck Inn, horses from the passenger and mail coaches were stabled, both on the north side and in a former courtyard at the front. In former days, the sheep farmers brought their wool here to be sold to wool merchants.

Several houses date from the early seventeenth century, and **Buckden Hall**, a large, three-storeyed Georgian building at the entrance to the village, probably stands on the site of a former manor house. **Buckden Bridge** was first built in 1689, and was rebuilt as a packhorse bridge in 1709 with money donated by the county for rebuilding the then more important bridge at Hubberholme which had been brought down by flood; in 1788 it was widened.

Again, the walking around here is tremendous: among other tracks, there is a footpath up to the summit of Buckden Pike, one by the river to Kettlewell, and a bridleway over the fell to Litton (formerly used by the parson from Arncliffe on his way to the Hubberholme chapelry); a good walk on the flanks of the Pike north of the village - the Rakes - is on the former Roman road from Ilkley to Bainbridge.

The right-hand fork out of Buckden leads through Cray and over the Kidstones Pass to Wensleydale via Bishopdale. We now take the left fork, which leads through Langstrothdale to the Fleet Moss route to Hawes in Wensleydale.

LANGSTROTHDALE. The Norman-founded Forest of Langstrothdale Chase was once a game and deer preserve governed by ancient Forest laws, with special privileges, penalties and courts. Langstrothdale (the name given to the uppermost stretch of Wharfedale) is Norse country (as the place names show), and some of the old Norse sheep farms became lodges for the foresters. These survive as the main hamlets of the dale: Cray, Hubberholme, Raisgill, Yockenthwaite, Deepdale, Beckermonds and Oughtershaw. The dale's name means 'the long stretch of ground, marshy and overgrown with brushwood' - as it would have been at that time.

Updale from Hubberholme, the woodland becomes gradually sparser until it disappears altogether, but the grandeur of this wild upland is incomparable. Here the now small river runs over successive shelves of limestone to form weirs, miniature gorges and rock pools.

HUBBERHOLME. This village actually consists of two hamlets - Hubberholme on the north side of the river by the church, and Kirk Gill on the south side. It is named after the Viking chieftain Hubba who helped to conquer this area.

Hubberholme Church, dedicated to St Michael and All Angels, was originally not a parish church as it is today, but a Forest chapel on a possible Anglo-Norse burial site. After the Dissolution of the Monasteries, the church was long served from the ancient parish of Arncliffe, especially by the curates at Halton Hill. It is said that at one time the sexton used to watch for the curate's white horse coming over the Horse Head Pass before ringing the bell to summon the congregation. This exquisite little church harmonizes beautifully with the dale, being built in local stone by local masons and roofed with lead from the Buckden mines. It is widely famous for its celebrated **rood loft,** one of the few surviving examples in the country, and only one of two in Yorkshire.

KETTLEWELL.
NEIL WINGATE.

Carved in oak and painted, red, black and yellow, it is remarkable for its late date, 1558. The date of the building itself is uncertain - there was probably a Saxon or even a Celtic church on this site - but the basis is mainly Transitional, of the twelfth century. The rounded arches of the south aisle might well date from this period, though they could simply be crude workmanship. The north aisle was probably added during the sixteenth century, when the windows were inserted. The short, unbuttressed Norman west tower has thirteenth- and sixteenth-century work; the porch bears the date 1696; and the font is heptagonal, probably Perpendicular, on an older (Norman?) stem. A bell dated 1601 stands on the floor. Extensive repairs and restoration were carried out in 1863 and in 1955–6, and the pews, choir stalls and chairs were made by Robert Thompson of Kilburn in 1934; his signature, the mouse, appears here and there on the woodwork.

The **George Inn** is actually in Kirk Gill and used to be the vicarage. Even as an inn it belonged to the church and was kept by the churchwarden until 1965. This is the scene of the traditional annual landletting on New Year's Day, locally known as the 'Hubberholme Parliament', perpetuating a custom nearly 1000 years old, when local farmers bid for the tenancy of a 16-acre field on Kirk Gill pasture (behind the inn) left in trust for the benefit of the parish poor. The vicar himself auctions the land on behalf of the church, and the money now goes to help old-age pensioners.

Hubberholme Bridge is of great interest, since in 1639 it was noted as being in decay, 'the said bridge leading between the markett towne of Lancaster and the markett towne of Newcastle-upon-Tyne' - evidence of the former importance attached to this road. The bridge was completely ruined by 1709 (when the new stone bridge was built at Buckden) and was rebuilt in 1734.

On the way to Yockenthwaite, we pass the farmhouse of **Raisgill**, like the other hamlets a former Forest lodge, and the start of the Horse Head Pass over to Halton Gill in Littondale.

YOCKENTHWAITE stands on the hillside above the narrow stone bridge leading to it. It was named after a Norse-Irishman, Eogan, and means 'Eogan's clearing in the forest'. This typically sited Norse settlement is now a tiny hamlet, but, after its period as a Forest lodge, there are records of other houses, an inn and a school. North-west of the village in a field across the river, a **Bronze age stone circle** is visible from the road, consisting of twenty stones standing on edge and forming a 25-foot-diameter circle, with four outlying stones in the north-west suggesting a double circle. A small mound at the centre indicates that this might have been an important burial site.

DEEPDALE is the next hamlet,where the iron road bridge of 1907 (replacing a stone packhorse bridge) crosses the river to a cluster of old farm buildings on the edge of a deep gill. It used to be much larger, with thirteen livings, including two inns and a blacksmith's, owing its importance to its position just off the packhorse road from Hawes over Fleet Moss and Horse Head Pass to Settle. On the west side of Deepdale Gill, about 1600 feet up, is the site of an Iron Age village with over twenty hut circles.

BECKERMONDS, the 'meeting of the becks', lies at the con-

STARBOTTON.

fluence of Oughtershaw and Greenfield Becks which together form the source of the Wharfe. Of Norse origin, and a former Forest lodge, the farms and fields were intaken from the surrounding commons. A school used to be held in the room over the porch of a building, now a barn, in the centre of the hamlet; the outside steps which led to it can still be traced. From this point, 1000 feet above sea level, an old bridle path follows Greenfield Beck to **Greenfield** and continues over the hills to Horton-in-Ribblesdale. The track is of monastic origin, since Greenfield was a grange of Fountains Abbey, and was also used as the packhorse route between Lancaster and the North-East (the route served by Hubberholme Bridge).

Turning right at Beckermonds, the road climbs by the side of Oughtershaw Beck to **Oughtershaw** at 1200 feet, where there is a nineteenth-century hall built by the Woodd family on the edge of a deep, wooded gorge. From here there is a track to **Cam Houses**, along the beckside through Swarthgill; but it is best to proceed as far as the summit of the road on Fleet Moss, where the lonely Cam Houses can be reached by a signposted green road, once the Roman road from Bainbridge to Ribblehead - the highest green road in Wharfedale, running below Dodd Fell along the extreme watershed of the Wharfe, from where there is the most spectacular panorama in Upper Wharfedale, overlooking, among the encircling mountains, the Three Peaks (Penyghent, Ingleborough and Whernside) and the very source of the Wharfe on Cam Fell.

Whether or not the visitor follows all or part of this track, it is at the top of Fleet Moss that our route ends, and we must now drive back down the same road as far as Hubberholme, where a short detour can be made to visit Cray, by crossing the bridge by the church, and taking the left fork to join the road from Buckden to Wensleydale.

CRAY is a tiny hamlet in Cray Gill, a former Norse settlement and then Forest lodge, at the foot of Kidstones Pass. Its former importance can be judged by the fact that there are many gaps between the present houses. At the White Lion Inn the antlers of the last deer to be killed in Langstrothdale can be seen, and near the hamlet are some magnificent waterfalls.

From Cray we head back down Wharfedale and at Kettlewell fork right to join the main road. Very shortly we arrive at Kilnsey.

KILNSEY. The most outstanding feature of Kilnsey is, of course, **Kilnsey Crag**, 'one of the natural wonders of Yorkshire' (Harry Speight), which dominates the dale at this point - in the words of Edmund Bogg (1904), its 'towering front bids defiance over the vale'! A notable landmark among the Great Scar Limestone scenery of the Dales, the crag was scoured out by the Wharfedale glacier during the last phases of the Ice Age. The crag itself is nearly 170 feet high to its summit from the road and overhangs 40 feet at the top. Springs gush out at its foot to form a clear beck which runs alongside the road on its way to the Wharfe. In front of the crag the flat fields are evidence of the silted-up lake left as the ice melted and the water was dammed by the moraine at Mill Scar Lash which stretches across the valley.

Kilnsey owes its importance, however, not to this spectacular natural feature, but to Fountains Abbey. Since it was

HUBBERHOLME
NEIL WINGATE

situated at the nearest convenient point to Fountains for managing their vast estates in Craven, and was also close to the ancient track which came from the abbey via Nidderdale and Dibble's Bridge, Hebden and Grassington, to Coniston, the principal grange for the Craven lands was created here between 1150 and 1175, with three resident lay brethren. The monastic track continues along Mastiles Lane (see p. 33) to Malham Moor and the Lake District. The grange was responsible for all the Fountains estates in Upper Wharfedale, Upper Airedale, Ribblesdale and Littondale, and Kilnsey Grange was built, together with a chapel, mills, houses and sheepfolds. Flocks of sheep were driven here for selling and shearing from Malham and the whole dale, and the wool was sent to Fountains Abbey for sale all over the country and on the Continent. After the Dissolution of the Monasteries, the property was sold and most of the monastic buildings were demolished.

However, on the site of the old grange, **Kilnsey Old Hall** was built in 1648 (as evidenced by the datestone). This three-storeyed, L-shaped structure with mullioned windows is a handsome example of seventeenth-century architecture. In front of the gable wall of the hall, at the entrance to the former courtyard, stands a small square outbuilding which is all that remains of the old grange's fifteenth-century gatehouse. It has a three-light window and above this the string course across the building shows the beginning of the semicircular arch which must have crossed the gateway.

Half a mile below Kilnsey, near **Mill Scar Lash**, were built two water mills in the sixteenth century, one a corn mill, where corn from all the Fountains Abbey lands in this part of Wharfedale was ground, and the other a fulling mill, where a portion of raw wool was spun and woven into cloth. There was also a smelt mill owned by Fountains which survived in some form until the mid-nineteenth century. On the flat area in front of the crag, the water meadows were used for growing rushes for thatching. All in all, Kilnsey must have once been a lively and busy centre.

The busiest event at Kilnsey now is **Kilnsey Show** which, first held in 1897, takes place on the level ground between the crag and the river on August Bank Holiday Tuesday. Apart from various competitions, sheepdog trials, and so forth, a major attraction is the Crag Race up the steep slope to the highest point and back.

On a more romantic level, it was from the now defunct inn, the Anglers Arms, that Dr Petty rode to meet his death at the hands of the Grassington murderer Tom Lee, by Grass Wood. The only inn here now is the Tennant Arms, a great angling centre.

Set back from the road on the right, just above Mill Scar Lash, is **Chapel House**, where the monks of Fountains Abbey formerly held possessions and perhaps a chapel. The west end of this Georgian building, now a guest house, is the oldest part, and within the grounds, a barn, formerly a house, has a datestone inscribed R 1613 T.

Slightly further down the valley, set back from the road on the left, is **Netherside Hall**, now used as a private school - a large old house perched high on a crag above a fine stretch of forest that descends precipitously to the edge of the river.

We shortly enter Threshfield and, bearing left, re-enter Grassington.

13 LITTONDALE

Car tour: allow 3 hours

Although a tributary valley, Littondale really belongs to Wharfedale, and is well worth a leisurely visit, not only because it is a very beautiful and unspoilt dale but also because it is interesting to compare its Great Scar Limestone, glacial landscape with that of Wharfedale, as well as discovering Littondale's own very personal character.

The River Skirfare flows through the dale to join the Wharfe above Kilnsey at the breached moraine at Amerdale Dub (the old name of Littondale being Amerdale). It is a U-shaped, flat-bottomed, glaciated valley, nine miles long, separated from Upper Wharfedale and Langstrothdale by a long mountain ridge on the north-east side, and furrowed on the south-west side by deep ravines fed by streams from Malham Moor and the mountains of Penyghent and Fountains Fell. On the valley floor the limestone walls form intricate patterns among the lush meadows: the irregular enclosures were being made from early times to the seventeenth century by both monks and farmers; and from the late eighteenth to the early nineteenth century the long, straight walls enclosing the common land in rectangles were built as a result of the Enclosure Acts. Iron Age habitations are scattered along the western fells, and well-marked strip lynchets indicate the site of former Anglian arable cultivation.

But Littondale's importance did not begin until after the Norman Conquest, when the Forest of Litton was created for the purpose of preserving and hunting game. Like the Forest of Langstrothdale (see p. 66), Litton was governed by special Forest laws, and down to the fourteenth century wolves, boars and deer roamed this valley. The next stage in the dale's development was when Richard de Percy granted most of Littondale to the monks of Fountains Abbey, who took over the land for grazing their sheep. Thus hunting and sheep farming comprise Littondale's main early history, for it was one of the few valleys almost untouched by leadmining. Since the end of the Norman Forest and the Dissolution of the Monasteries, the way of life in Littondale has changed little over the centuries: now it is still mainly devoted to agriculture.

To reach Littondale by car, we take the main road from Threshfield through Kilnsey (see p. 70), and, passing Kilnsey Crag, avoid the first turn-off to the left, crossing over the Skirfare Bridge and turning left on to the direct road to Hawkswick.

HAWKSWICK. Since many birds of prey were apparently common to this dale in earlier times, it is probable that this village was named after the hawks that must have nested nearby in the cliffs. (The other possibility is that it was named after a Viking warrior, as the ending -wick is a Norse one, meaning village.) The houses are built of limestone in various styles, and the older properties are near the river. Behind the village is a track up the fellside leading eventually over Knipe into Kettlewell. On the lower slopes are Anglian cultivation terraces - evidence of the settlement's early foundations.

If we now cross Hawkswick bridge, a lane bends round to join the main route to Arncliffe, where we bear right, shortly passing on the left **Arncliffe Cote** and **Hawkswick Cote,** which face each other across a small valley (Cote Gill): these were former granges of Fountains Abbey and are still sheep farms. A little further along, the road runs below **Blue Scar,** an area of limestone clints on the summit of which are many remains of an important Iron Age settlement. We enter the village of Arncliffe through an avenue of sycamore trees.

ARNCLIFFE is the largest village in the dale, well sited on a gravel delta above the flood level of the river, and sheltering beneath the craggy mass of Arncliffe Clowder where the limestone scars break through the trees on the ridges. It is a perfect example of an Anglian planned village, consisting of a spacious green round which are gathered the main buildings; behind these are small crofts, roughly one to each house. Common pastures spread along the terraces of the limestone fells up to the base of the gritstone heather moorland above. Traces of even earlier settlement can be seen in the 'Celtic field system' south of the village, with circular and rectangular stone enclosures, the lower courses of which still stand. Like Hawkswick, Arncliffe probably owes its name to the presence of birds of prey in former times (from Anglo-Saxon *earn*, eagle); it is possible that eagles once nested in the limestone scars above the village.

There are several walks from Arncliffe: a riverside path leads through the fields up to Litton and down to Hawkswick; near the Falcon Inn, an old monastic road climbs the side of Cowside Gill to Malham Tarn, a green road which once connected the Fountains Abbey granges at Malham with those at Arncliffe; on the opposite side of the valley two

KILNSEY CRAG.

tracks lead over the ridge to Kettlewell and to Starbotton (the old market road from Settle).

At the far end of the green, by Cowside Beck, is **Arncliffe Mill,** an old water-powered corn mill owned in the fourteenth century by the Augustinian canons of Bolton, rebuilt and turned into a cotton mill around 1820, closed in 1875, and finally reduced from its original four storeys and converted into flats.

Attractively situated on the riverside by the bridge stands **Arncliffe Church** (St Oswald's). There has probably been a church on this site since Saxon times; a Norman stone-built church of around 1100 was rebuilt in 1796 and further remodelled and restored in 1841, from when the body of the church mostly dates, apart from the Perpendicular west tower, a survival from the fifteenth century. On a wall inside the church is a list of the men who fought at Flodden Field in 1513. Its parish at one time included not only the chapel-of-ease at Halton Gill but also the church at Hubberholme, to which the Arncliffe incumbent had to ride, over the 2000-foot fells from Litton.

Across the bridge, the lovely house set back on the left is **Bridge End,** where Charles Kingsley spent some time during his stay at Malham Tarn House. Part of the *Water Babies* was written here, and includes descriptions of Littondale (called Vendale in the book).

Joining the road from Hawkswick, we bear left and suddenly, just round a right-hand bend, we come upon a superb example of a yeoman's house, **Old Cote,** bearing the date-stone 1650. The projecting porch has a stepped three-light window, and in the left angle between the porch and the house is a staircase turret; the other windows are mullioned. This well-proportioned house is one of the architectural delights of the area.

LITTON is two miles updale from Arncliffe, a small, mainly linear group of grey stone cottages and farmhouses, with one inn, the Queens Arms. Since the old Settle market road forded the river at Litton, a number of tracks meet here, many providing good walks: one track leads over the ridge to Buckden in Wharfedale; and a green road crosses the river to slant steeply up the opposite fellside, keeping parallel to Penyghent Gill, with striking prospects of Penyghent itself, until it joins the road from Halton Gill to Stainforth.

Towards Halton Gill, at the point where the Hesleden Beck joins the Skirfare, if we look left up the wooded ravine that joins Penyghent Gill, we see a magnificent view of Penyghent at the back.

HALTON GILL, two miles up the dale, is a cluster of mainly seventeenth-century houses tucked away at a height of 1000 feet at the foot of the Horse Head Pass, a bridleway to Raisgill in Langstrothdale, once part of the packhorse trail from Hawes to Settle, and now one of the finest walks in Yorkshire. From the summit of Horse Head Moor is a vast panorama of the Three Peaks (Ingleborough, Penyghent and Whernside) as well as most of the notable heights of Wharfedale. In the days of the packhorse road, Littondale was a busy and important highway, and Halton Gill a frequent stopping place for trains of packhorses. Over the last 200 years it has steadily diminished to become little more than a remote hamlet.

Of the buildings of note, the old hall in the centre of the

ARNCLIFFE.

NEIL WINGATE.

village, built in 1641, contains an oak staircase. More important is the church of **St John the Baptist**, a curious structure comprising a church and schoolhouse under one roof, sharing the same bell-cote. It is not known exactly when the church was built, but Saxton's map of 1577 marks 'Hawtongill chap.' Certainly the church was rebuilt in 1626, when the dated schoolhouse on the west end was added, and was much remodelled in 1848. Until 1847 the resident curate combined his office with that of schoolmaster, living upstairs and teaching in the schoolroom downstairs. The school was closed in 1958. Since for most of its history this chapel-of-ease to Arncliffe had its own curate, it was often he who officiated at Hubberholme, crossing over the Horse Head Pass; the most famous of these was Thomas Lindley, who used to ride over on a white horse, clearly visible from Hubberholme Church.

Half a mile up the road from Halton Gill lies **Foxup**, a tiny hamlet nestling peacefully by Foxup Beck which with Cosh Beck together form the source of the Skirfare. Fountains Abbey once had a sheep farm here. A track leads on the right of Cosh Beck along the very watershed of the Skirfare to **Cosh**, a lonely farmhouse surrounded by an area of unenclosed moors drained by the rivulets of the beck; there is no track out of the head of Littondale, so Cosh is the furthest we can go in our exploration of this dale. Throughout the head of the valley are many Iron Age remains - small hutments and fields; and in monastic times this now deserted tract of country was moderately populated.

We now return to Halton Gill, where we have the choice of either returning to Arncliffe by the same road, or else taking a more exciting but longer route skirting Malham Moor. From Halton Gill we take the Stainforth road forking right out of the village and crossing the bridge to mount Hesleden Bergh. Just before the highest point of this stretch of road, it is well worth looking back for the marvellous sight of Halton Gill sheltering under Horse Head Moor, as well as of the steep-sided U-shape of Littondale. The road now leads above Penyghent Gill, offering splendid views of Penyghent and Fountains Fell. About 500 yards past the second house on this road (Penyghent House) is **Giant's Grave**, a large gravel mound in which some stones set on edge can still be seen in a few places, though most of the larger stones have been taken away by farmers. However, this stone circle must have been an important burial site for a sizeable late Stone Age community.

In less than four miles we fork left by Sannet Hall and, avoiding three right-hand forks, pass close by **Malham Tarn**, a glacial lake remaining from the Ice Age, where there is a good nature trail. Following the road through Darnbrook, we climb Nab End and descend equally steeply on the left of **Cowside Beck**, a deep and most spectacular gorge.

On reaching Arncliffe, we bear right and, keeping to the right-hand side of the valley, pass Arncliffe and Hawkswick Cotes to continue on this road. Above us, at a height of about 1300 feet, is **Doukabottom Cave**, where many remains of prehistoric man were excavated, mainly of the Iron Age and some from Roman times, as well as older remains of Arctic animals from the later stages of the Ice Age. At the junction of the Kettlewell road, we bear right and follow the route described in Chapter 12 through Kilnsey and back to Grassington.

14 STUMP CROSS & PARCEVAL HALL

Car tour plus visits: allow 2½ hours

Some of the most fantastic limestone caves in the country, an old mining field, a beautifully restored Elizabethan hall and a gorge haunted by a spectral hound are visited here.

Taking the road through Hebden (see p. 36), we cross **Dibble's Bridge**. Lying on an old monastic route (see p. 72), the steepness of the road and the narrowness of the gully make this a dramatic (and dangerous) landmark. On the right, just over two miles further on, are **Stump Cross Caverns**, named after the stump of the former Craven Cross. The underground caves display weirdly beautiful stalactites and calcite formations glittering in the hidden coloured lights, and are named after individual features - the Jewel Box, the Chamber of Pillars, the Cathedral, and so on.

Further up the road is one of the highest villages in England, **Greenhow**, at about 1300 feet, with a panorama of Nidderdale and the surrounding moorlands. A centre of leadmining until the late nineteenth century, Greenhow is now a remote hamlet with one inn, the Miners Arms. Greenhow Hill is an extension of the Grassington mining field (see p. 18); the leadmining's beginnings are evidenced by the two pigs of Greenhow lead bearing Roman inscriptions of the first century AD. Now the only remains are the wide scatter of miners' cottages (many in ruins), the disused shafts and spoil heaps. **St Mary's Church,** built in 1857, is believed to be the highest church in Yorkshire.

Leaving Greenhow, we return towards Hebden, forking left at Fancarl House to **Skyreholme**, a scattered hamlet of Anglian origins. Turning sharp left at Skyreholme, we pass the disused paper mill which once had an enormous water wheel supplied by a dam in the mouth of Trollers Gill. We soon fork left on to a lane leading to **Parceval Hall**. This lovely former yeoman's farmhouse, first mentioned in 1535 documents, has seventeenth-century additions and was restored and extended in 1928 by Sir William Milner, who constructed a private chapel and terraced gardens, rockeries and nurseries, stocked with rare plants and occasionally open to the public. In 1963 the house was opened as an Anglican retreat and conference centre. It is reputed to have once hidden the seventeenth-century highwayman, William Nevison, the source of many Dick Turpin legends.

On the opposite side of the beck a track leads to **Trollers Gill**, the right-hand valley of the Y-shape, through which there is no right-of-way. This splendid dry limestone gorge resembles Gordale Scar in miniature; in fact a fourteenth-century survey refers to 'Gordale in Appletreewick'. With its overhanging cliffs and its boulder-strewn valley floor, it has readily lent itself to romance, its name implying connections with the trolls of Norse legends. The most extravagant myth is that of the Barguest, the phantom hound who is supposed to have his lair here, variously described as being as large as a small bear, with bared fangs and eyes as big as saucers, or 'shaggy, wolfish and of diabolic aspect' (Edmund Bogg).

The return route is via Skyreholme and Appletreewick, taking the Skuff road as in Chapter 10.